William Edgar Simonds

Practical suggestions on the sale of patents,

With forms of assignment, license, contract, power of attorney to sell,

rights

William Edgar Simonds

Practical suggestions on the sale of patents,
With forms of assignment, license, contract, power of attorney to sell, rights

ISBN/EAN: 9783337814649

Printed in Europe, USA, Canada, Australia, Japan

Cover: Foto ©ninafisch / pixelio.de

More available books at **www.hansebooks.com**

PRACTICAL SUGGESTIONS

ON THE

SALE OF PATENTS,

WITH

FORMS OF ASSIGNMENT, LICENSE, CONTRACT, POWER OF ATTORNEY TO SELL RIGHTS, &c. MANY OF THEM ORIGINAL,

AND

INSTRUCTIONS RELATIVE THERETO,

WITH

HINTS UPON INVENTION,

AND THE

UNITED STATES CENSUS.

BY WM. EDGAR SIMONDS,
ATTORNEY AT LAW, SOLICITOR OF PATENTS.

PUBLISHED BY THE AUTHOR.
HARTFORD, CONN.
1871.

STANDARD ASSOCIATION, PRINTERS,
Bridgeport, Conn.

PREFACE.

Having had occasion, during some years of Patent practice, to observe the blind way in which the large majority of inventors grope about, in the vain endeavor to sell their patents, and also having had the opportunity of observing the methods followed by business men, in dealing with the same inventions, it has occurred to the writer that he could, possibly, render a service to a large class of men, with whose interests his own work has been, and is to be identified, by collecting together the results of these various observations, and giving them form and sequence on a printed page.

It is certain to the mind of the writer, that inventions which are really improvements, have a financial value, just as surely as any article of trade, and that the main difficulty in disposing of them arises from the fact that, generally, the men who have them for sale do not know just how to make a clear statement of the value of their inventions, nor to whom to present such statement, when made.

This little work is an attempt to point out, in a simple way, the methods to achieve such results.

With respect to the forms for assignment, license and contract, and the advice given with reference thereto, the writer feels sure they will be of value to inventors and owners of patents, for he has found them reliable and convenient in practice.

The "Hints upon Invention" may possibly help some inventors, who are misdirecting their energies, to a clearer view as to how they may make their endeavors profitable.

If this little volume shall serve, in any measure, the purposes for which it is intended, the author's ambition with reference thereto will be satisfied.   W. E. S.

PRELIMINARY.

Having made a really meritorious invention, and having secured a patent thereupon, the battle of the inventor, who would sell his patent, is but just begun. Heretofore he may have done some good skirmishing, but now he must face the music of solid battle.

All along till now, from the first crude conception of the invention, on through its various stages of trial and experiment, till the device stands forth completed, and yet on through the ordeal of the Patent Office, till its parchment, ribbon and seal assure the inventor of its protection, he is usually sustained by an enthusiasm which suffuses his whole being with its rosy flush. In a sort of vague way, it has, all along, seemed to him that when his patent should issue, his labors would be done, and he would thenceforth rest on his well earned laurels. Not that the situation has thus stood forth in his mind, clearly and sharply defined, for it rarely occurs to an inventor to seriously consider upon what will be the state of affairs at this juncture, till the progress of events brings him to it, but the cloud which hovered over this bit of promised land roughly assumed this shape.

When the inventor has finally received his patent, and read and re-read it some dozens of times, it begins to occur to him that he will just thrust in his sickle and reap a little of the golden harvest, which imagination has, all along, been sowing for him. Plainly, he looks around for a purchaser, and with a kind of astonishment, waking up, as it were, from a dream, he finds that purchasers do not stand around ready to exchange their filthy lucre for his invention. Generally unaccustomed to the ways of business and of business men, he finds himself, in a short time, as helpless in his endeavors as can well be imagined. He does not know what class of men will be most likely to take an interest in his invention, nor how to reach them, nor what to say to them. Not rarely, after a year or so of this blind groping, disgust with the whole thing sets in, and the inventor renounces this and all other inventions forever.

This has been the experience, over and over again, of thousands upon thousands of inventors, and in multitudes of cases where a purchaser has been found, the invention has been sold to him for a song, and the buyer, applying business principles to the management of the invention, has realized the lion's share of the money from it.

The Patent Office Reports are full of useful devices, which have never been introduced into the markets of trade, and which, it is easy to say, would have netted their inventors considerable sums of money, if they had been properly brought out in their time.

It is partly with the purpose of indicating to this class of inventors to whom they should present their patents for sale, and how to present them, that this work has been projected.

It must not be supposed that all inventions are salable, or that the directions hereinafter contained are infallible! Some inventions are very far from being improvements, for though they may be very ingenious, yet they are neither simpler, more efficient or cheaper than the common devices in use for the same purpose, and consequently there is no money in them. Such inventions may sometimes be sold to men with more money than good judgment, yet the cases where this can occur are so few, that it is not worth while to place any dependence upon them.

It is, however, believed that a person will rarely fail to dispose of an invention of any merit, if he takes the pains to understand and intelligently act upon the suggestions hereinafter contained.

PATENT BROKERS.

Almost, if not quite, every issue of various scientific and mechanical periodicals are adorned with the advertisements of parties who hold themselves out as making a business of buying and selling patents, almost always strictly " on commission." The following, omitting names and localities, is the actual advertisement of such a party, as it appeared from week to week :

"*PATENT RIGHTS SOLD ON COMMISSION,*
And Valuable Inventions introduced by the most experienced Patent Salesmen in the Union. * * * No CHARGE FOR OUR SERVICES, UNLESS SUCCESSFUL," *etc.*

This is a fair sample of a whole class of advertisements.

A letter addressed to one of these advertisers elicited the following reply :

" *Dear Sir :*
Your favor of the 2d is received. We charge from $50 to $250 for expenses of negotiating Patents, and 10 to 15 per cent for commission. Yours, truly, _____ _____."

A letter sent to another elicited the following reply :

Dear Sir :
Your favor of the 7th is received. We have been so taken up with other matters, have scarcely had time to reply. Our terms require the patentee to furnish $100, with which to advertise his patent, furnish one perfect model or drawing, and allow us forty-five days within which to make the sale," etc., etc.
Yours, Respectfully, _____ _____.

Similar answers were received to letters written to others of these brokers. They were invariably accompanied by circulars, describing in glowing terms the advantages the senders were able to offer. There was a striking similarity among these circulars, and, in one case, two were found, parts of which were identically the same, word for word, although they issued from offices more than a thousand miles apart.

It will be observed that these patent brokers always advertise to sell *on commission*. Their letters and circulars disclose that there is always an advance fee, varying from $25.00 to $250.00, which can hardly be said to be in conformity with the terms of the advertisements. Commission houses engaged in the sale of other articles always pay their own expenses, and not unfrequently advance money upon goods consigned them, before they are sold. For a patent broker to first advertise to sell patents on commission, and then, afterwards, to charge an advance fee, ought, at least, to subject him to suspicion.

Another thing—it is difficult to see what advantages a patent broker can have over the patentee, if the latter is once made acquainted with the way to reach probable customers. The broker certainly cannot understand the nature of the invention better than the inventor, and besides, as the buyer well knows that the broker must have a large commission from the price realized, he has an incentive to buy from the inventor, and save this commission.

The broker will probably claim—

First, that by education and experience, he is better qualified than inventors in general, to set forth the advantages of the invention, and the profits to be derived therefrom ; and,

Second, that he keeps an open office, at a settled place, where a person seeking investments in patents may come, examine, and select.

To the first argument it may be replied, that the ability to well set forth the advantages of an invention is not necessarily incident to the occupation of a patent broker ; and to the second argument it may be replied that the legitimate market for inventions is found among those who are engaged in manufacturing or selling articles akin to the invention on sale, and that this class of men will, as a rule, display their usual shrewdness, and much prefer to deal with the inventor, at first hand, and thus save the heavy commission, which they well know the broker must receive.

The sum of money which these brokers require as an advance fee, will, in most cases, pay all the expense of presenting an invention to all that class of persons who will be likely to buy it, which is all that the brokers will promise to do, and the invention is, meanwhile, entirely within the control of the inventor.

These remarks are based upon the supposition that the advance fee paid to the broker is wholly and honestly appropriated for advertising, etc., about which a person is justified in entertaining grave doubts.

At any rate, it is better for the inventor to wait till he has exhausted all the unequivocal resources at command, before resorting to this.

PREREQUISITES.

1. MODELS.

It is absolutely necessary, in offering a patented invention for sale, to have one or more perfect working models. If the invention is a machine, and not too large and costly, and it is within the inventor's means, he should construct, or have constructed, at least one full sized machine that will work to perfection. If, beyond question, the machine is too costly to allow of the inventor's building one, then he should have in its place complete, artistic drawings in elevation, plan and detail.

In making a model, it is not enough to construct a rude device, which, in a halting and awkward way, will illustrate the principle of the improvement. The machine should be most carefully and perfectly made. The mass of minds will much more readily understand and appreciate the *principle* of the machine if the mechanical execution is perfect. Whatever the after made machines may be, the first one should be as near perfect as possible. The inventor will usually find that, at his best, he will have enough to apologize for, without being responsible for poor workmanship. It is much easier to interest a crowd in a fine piece of mechanism, even if the device be old, than in a new but roughly made invention. The tea, coffee and spice merchants understand this, and take advantage of it, when they put in their windows handsome specimens of small steam engines, which are supposed to be always grinding fragrant Mocha or Old Java, the merchants well knowing that half the people who go by will take a look at the polished and painted machinery, and will thereby be drawn to look at their merchandise,

If the invention is a small article, as a shirt stud, a mouse trap, a toy, or a clothes line holder, it is best for the inventor to have quite a number made, that he may send samples to those who may become interested in the invention, if it should be found desirable. If the invention is a new compound, or a new process, the inventor must provide materials, etc., for explaining and illustrating the process, or the effects of the new compound.

2. FIRST COST.

Another necessity, in offering a patent for sale, is to be able to show just what the first cost of the article is. If the invention is some complicated and costly machine, the inventor must show, either from his own knowledge, or the calculations of some competent person, what is its first cost.

A competent person would be a civil or mechanical engineer, or a machinist, or other mechanic of experience in constructing other machines of the same general nature. If a responsible party can be found, who will agree to furnish the machine well made, for some certain sum apiece, this is an important item to be had.

If the invention is some small device, and not costly, the inventor should have some dozens, or, better still, a few hundreds of them made, so as to get at the exact first cost. To find a responsible party, who will undertake to make the articles for a certain sum per hundred, per gross, or per thousand, is also important here. The difference of two or three cents, in the first cost of small articles of general use, often determines who shall command the market; in other words, who shall make money from the manufacture, and who shall lose.

If the invention is a new process, the inventor must be amply prepared to show the cost of his process, as compared with that in common use for the same, or similar purpose.

3. THE PROFIT

The profit made on a single article is, of course, the difference between the first cost and the retail price at which it is finally sold to the consumer. To determine the amount of this profit upon a new invention is a necessary thing, before offering it for sale. The whole profit is divided into three, and sometimes four parts, viz. the manufacturer's profit, the wholesale dealer's profit, and the retail dealer's profit. The manufacturer sells to the wholesale dealer, the wholesale dealer to the retail dealer, and he to the consumer. There is, sometimes, intermediate between the manufacturer and wholesale dealer, the jobber, but the writer fails to see the use of such an intermediate, and if he is made use of, his profit should be a per centage on the profit of the manufacturer, so that in making the division of profits, it is not necessary to consider the jobbber at all. The retail price of the article should be fixed as is commensurate with the allowance of fair profits to each of these parties. If the invention is an improvement upon an article in common use, as for instance a flat iron, and the first cost of the article is not greater than the first cost of the common article, then it is probably best to adopt just the scale of profits which obtains in the trade with regard to the common article. An inquiry put to a friendly dealer in the articles upon which the invention is an improvement, will elicit what these profits are. If the first cost is somewhat greater, then the retail price should be correspondingly advanced, the scale of profits being kept at about the same ratio of correspondence. If the first cost is less than that of the common article, it is probably advisable to keep the retail price up to that of the common article, and thus give larger profits.

There is no general correspondence of profits to these three parties, on different articles. The profits on different manufactures differ widely, and with no reference whatever to a common standard. The only rule that can be given, in this regard, is, to ascertain the scale of prices and profits which prevail from the manufacturer to the consumer, in the trade, upon articles which are nearest like the invention under consideration, and then to assimilate, as far as possible, the profits upon the new article to this scale, varying, however, as any good reason may dictate. If the invention is a new process, the inventor must be prepared to show the gain in using the new process, as compared with the old, and the increased profit secured thereby. The same is true, if the invention is a new machine for producing an old article, as, for instance, drain tile.

4. THE MARKET.

Having ascertained the first cost of producing the article invented, and having fixed upon the profit to be derived from a single article, the next step is to enquire how extensive a market is offered to the invention.

If it is an invention useful to both sexes, to children and adults alike, it will have for a market the whole population of the United.States, over thirty-eight millions of souls. If useful to adult males only, the market will be about one-fourth of this number. This thirty-eight millions of population is composed, roughly, of males and females in about equal proportions, and each of these divisions is composed of about one-half adults and one-half children, so that, if the invention appeals to persons irrespective of their avocations, the market for it is readily computed. If the invention is one which will be useful in every family, the market will be about one-eighth the whole number of souls, as on an average there are about eight persons in a family.

The full census report for 1870 will probably contain such full statistics of the different trades, professions and callings of the people of the United States, that there can be readily gathered from it how many there are of any class or classes of persons to whom an invention may be of particular utility, and the whole of such class or classes will constitute the market for the invention.

Instead of being directly useful to any class of persons, an invention may be an improvement in the manufacture of some article, as flour barrels, for instance, and then it is necessary to ascertain the actual annual production of this article in the country; or, it may be an improved process, say of smelting iron, and then it is necessary to find how many tons of iron are annually smelted. The census of 1870 will be a great aid in ascertaining most, if not all of this information, but when it is deficient, the librarian of almost any public library can direct an inventor where to find the desired statistics. The wants which inventions are designed to fill are so various, and the statistics which would answer all such enquiries fill so many pages, that it is impracticable to more than direct, in this book, as to what information is needed.

14

One element which must be taken into account in determining the extent of the market for a new invention, if it is an article and not a process, is its durability. If the article, when once sold to the consumer, will last him for ten years, of course the market for that article is not so large as it would be, if, in the natural course of things, it would last but a short time, and then would require to be renewed. Having ascertained the extent of the market for a new invention, the gross profit to be derived from it can be readily computed, by multiplying the profit upon a single article by the whole number which may probably be sold.

5. CAPITAL REQUIRED.

If the amount of capital required to develop an invention, and introduce it to the public, is small, this will be an additional argument to use in selling.

6. PRICE TO BE ASKED.

This is a matter, for determining which no absolute and definite rule can be given. It is pretty safe to say that inventors are rather apt to overestimate than underestimate the value of their inventions, Of course, the more profit there is to be made from an invention, and the larger market there is for it, the more valuable it is. If it appeals to but a small and widely dispersed class, its value will be less. If it is a new and radical improvement in the manufacture of some staple article, as iron or steel, like the Bessemer process, for instance, a half million dollars would be a moderate price for it. If a meritorious improvement on some household article in general use, or some article of dress, or a new and amusing toy, a few thousands might be a fair price. Again, if a really valuable improvement in some important agricultural implement, as a reaper or mower, from twenty to fifty thousand dollars would probably not be exorbitant. In no case can an inventor expect to get but a fraction of the value of his invention, as shown by the gross profit to be derived from it, for he must be able to offer the lion's share of this profit to the purchaser, as an inducement to buy ; and, besides, the purchaser will have the trouble and risk of making this profit piecemeal, as it were, from the actual use and sale of the invention, The advice of friends who are in business, especially if their business is such as to make them conversant with the market for the device under consideration, will be of great value in fixing the asking price for a patent. Having fixed upon this asking price, it is then quite safe to lessen it by at least one-fourth of its amount, and on this basis proceed.

7. THE VALUE OF PARTS OF A PATENT.

Having fixed upon the gross sum to be asked for the whole of a patent, it is very easy to determine the value of territorial rights under the same. If the whole value of a patent is ten thousand dollars, a state right will be worth just such a part of the whole, as its population bears ratio to the population of the whole country. Take, for instance, the State of Connecticut. Its population is about five hundred and forty thousand, while the whole population of the United States is about thirty-eight millions. The value of the right for this State will be arithmetically expressed thus . $\frac{540,000}{38,000,000}$ of $10,000=$142.00 ; or, not to put too fine a point upon it, $150.00. But the inventor cannot afford to sell one state at the same rate that he would sell all the states in a lump. The price for a single state should be double of the exact proportion which the one State bears to all the States together, so that the price of the State of Connecticut would be three hundred dollars. This rule, however, should not be stringently applied to any of the Gulf States, nor to any state west of Missouri, except California, for the reason that these excepted states are not as much interested in manufacturing as are their sister states, and for some other reasons, do not offer as good markets.

An advance of fifty per cent over the value, as determined by the population, is enough to put upon these excepted states. No advance whatever, over this value, should be asked for territories. Having ascertained the value of a state in this manner, the value of a single county can be determined in precisely the same way, first finding the value as determined by the ratio the population of the county bears to the population of the whole state, and then doubling the sum. The value of a town may be determined in precisely the same way from the value of a county. The census of the United States, taken in Eighteen Hundred and Seventy, by states and counties, will be found further along. Those who desire to sell rights for towns, will have to procure the more extended census report for this purpose.

8. SHOP RIGHTS.

A "shop right," so called, is the right to use the patent or manufacture under it, at some shop or manufactory; it may be restricted to a certain place, or left unrestricted. It cannot be considered advisable to make sales of this kind under a patent, unless there are strong reasons why the territory should not be sold. As such a right, when no royalty is reserved, is liable to abuse, it is very difficult to fix upon the value of it, for although a factory may have been doing but a small business, previous to the purchase of the shop right, the factory may thereafter expand its business, so as to practically interfere with sales under the patent in all parts of the country.

A shop right should be limited to a certain annual production and to a certain place. If this is not done, an effort should be made to ascertain the annual production of the factory to which the sale is to be made, as compared with the like product of the whole country, and then a proportionate price should be fixed upon the shop right, doubling the value as shown by the computation, in the same manner as was directed for fixing the value of state rights.

There are some kinds of patents under which it may be advisable to sell shop rights; as, for instance, an improvement in the manufacture of steel. The greater part of all the establishments for making steel will be found congregated in three or four manufacturing centers, and the proper and sensible way of making such a patent available to them, is to sell them each a shop right. It is not difficult, in such cases, to ascertain the amount of the annual production of each establishment, and this amount, as compared with the whole annual production of the whole country, will furnish the basis for computing the value of the shop right, provided, of course, that the gross price for the whole patent has already been fixed upon.

9. ROYALTIES.

A royalty is a duty paid by one who uses the patent of another, at a certain rate for each article or quantity manufactured, or a per centage upon the sales. This method of realizing from a patent is, perhaps, the commonest of any, and if the patent is a valuable one, and the party who manufactures the article acts in good faith, it is generally the most profitable for the patentee in the long run. On the other hand, if the patent is of doubtful merit, the patentee better sell it outright, and it will be best in any case, if a fair price can be realized, for both parties to the negotiation will then be freed from any danger of injury happening to them from the bad faith of the other party.

The royalty to be asked, where a patent is let out in this way, differs very much with the article which is the subject of the patent. If the patent is an improvement upon an article of staple manufacture, it is best to keep the retail price as low as possible, and to effect this, the royalty must be low, varying from three to five per cent of the amount of the sales. On large and heavy machinery, from five to eight per cent of the selling price is perhaps a fair charge. On agricultural machinery, from six to nine would not be unreasonable. On small articles of jewelry, fancy articles, toys, dress, etc., etc., a royalty amounting to ten per cent of the gross sales is not too much. In any case, it is not best to leave the manufacturer free to make as many or as few as he chooses of the article, for he may choose to make none, and then the patentee will get nothing, and the manufacturer will still retain his license. All agreements upon royalty should contain a clause that if a manufacturer shall not pay royalty upon a certain minimum number, the patentee shall have the option of declaring the license null and void.

Forms of this kind will be found further on. All such agreements should also contain a condition, that at stated times the manufacturer shall render to the patentee a true and exact account of all the patented articles made and sold by him, since the last account and payment, to which account the patentee shall have the right to require the oath of the manufacturer, and that if then the patentee is not satisfied, he shall have the right to view the manufacturer's books.

If one manufacturer will undertake to supply the whole market, and will fix the minimum royalty which he must pay sufficiently high, then it is best to let him have the sole right to manufacture ; but if it becomes necessary to let the patent out to more than one, then the minimum amount of royalty should be fixed upon the same general principle as followed in determining the value of a shop right.

TO WHOM TO OFFER THE PATENT AND HOW TO OFFER IT.

Having settled all these preliminary matters, and having become acquainted with the nature of the various kinds of rights which it is usual to dispose of under patents, the next question to be answered, is, "What class of persons will be the most likely to buy the patent, or rights under it." To this the answer is plain. If it is an article in distinction from a process, it is likely to be most readily sold to some one of that class of manufacturers who are making articles of the same class as this. " How to get the names and addresses of all of such a class ?" Answer—there are men in New York and other large cities, who make it their business to furnish, for a reasonable consideration, full and complete lists of all parties engaged in any particular trade, occupation, profession, or manufacture throughout the country. The inventor has, let us suppose, devised a new and useful article of jewelry for gentlemen, say a shirt stud or sleeve button. He, of course, will naturally expect to sell his patent to some manufacturing jeweller, and accordingly he will procure, from one of these agents referred to, a list of all such parties, either in some particular part of the country, or in the whole country.

It is not generally, advisable to procure more than a partial list, at first, because a sale may be made to one of these, and if not, then the list can be readily enlarged, from time to time, as may become desirable.

Having procured such a list of parties, the next thing is to properly present the thing to them, one by one and for this purpose it is advisable to prepare a circular, bearing a good "cut" of the invention, if it be susceptible of such illustration, and containing a concise, but very careful description of the invention and its operation, setting forth its advantages over the common article, or process, on which it is an improvement. It should contain a careful statement of the actual first cost of the article or process, supported by facts and figures, and offers of responsible parties, if any have been made, to manufacture at such prices. It should also show what a reasonable retail price would be, as governed by the margins which obtain in the trade for similar articles, and from this deduce the profit to be made on a single specimen. It should further show, by actual statistics, taken from reliable sources, how extensive a market is offered to the invention, taking into account the average life of the article and the whole duration of the patent, and from this should be computed the whole sum to be realized, if the whole market is supplied. This figure will always be a large one, and after making this computation, it is advisable to say, in substance, as follows;—" even if but one-half or one-fourth of the whole market is actually supplied, the gross profit will be," etc., etc. which, being a reasonable supposition, can hardly fail to carry weight. If the claim in the patent is a strong one, it is best to insert it in the circular, and call attention to its strength.

It is, probably, not best to put into the circular the terms upon which the patent, or rights under it, will be sold. That can be better set forth in a letter to accompany the circular. The following circular, founded upon an imaginary "Improved Collar Stud," will illustrate the general method to be followed in preparing such a circular.

Improved Collar Stud.

LETTERS PATENT NO. 100,010. DATED JUNE 6, 1871.

This is an indispensable article of a gentleman's toilet. It is not only a perfect collar stud, but an equally perfect tie holder. All who have ever worn a "snap" or butterfly tie—and this comprises all American *mankind*—are well aware of the vexations incident to fastening the loop of these ties over the common shirt button, or collar stud. Many a hasty, if not profane, ejaculation has been the result of attempting this task. It has often been a matter of equal disgust for a gentleman—a wearer of one of these ties—on reaching home, to find that he has been bravely marching through the streets, minus a neck-tie, which has, in an unlucky moment, escaped the faithless grasp of the common button, or stud.

This little device completely cures these troubles. The loop of a tie is as readily slipped into one of the little hooks, upon the front of the stud, as a hat is hung on a nail, and it cannot escape therefrom by accident.

The owner of the patent, which has a broad and strong claim, is not in circumstances which will allow him to undertake the introduction and sale of the studs. He will, therefore, dispose of the patent, or rights under it, and asks attention to the following remarks, which show its great value.

FIRST COST.—It is made of gold plated sheet metal, commonly known among manufacturing jewelers as "stock plate," and all the parts are struck up by dies, so that it can be made very cheaply, at a cost not exceeding five cents apiece. Messrs. Brazos & Copperman, of Waterbury, Conn., and also Mr. Chas. Ringman, of North Attleboro, Mass., have offered to make them, in quantities. at that price. Of course, if these parties can furnish the studs at that price, the real cost is less, for manufacturers do not generally carry on their business for fun or philanthropy.

THE RETAIL PRICE.—Plated collar studs, of the common kinds, sell at retail prices varying all the way from twenty-five cents to one dollar, according to plate and workmanship. No stud, which is as well plated as this, sells for less than fifty cents, and as these last are merely the common kind, with no improvements, fifty cents would be a reasonable retail price for this improved stud, giving, as the profit on a single article, forty-five cents. This allows the manufacturer to sell to the jobber for ten cents apiece, a profit of one hundred per cent ; the jobber to the wholesale dealer for fifteen cents, a profit of fifty per cent ; the wholesale dealer to the retailer at twenty-five cents, a profit of sixty-six and two-thirds per cent ; and the retail dealer to the consumer at fifty cents, a profit of one hundred per cent ; so that while the retail price is not higher than for the common article, the profits of all concerned are enormous, and will make it a favorite with the trade.

THE MARKET.—Of the 38,000,000 of people in the United States, about one-fourth, 9,500,000, are men, and about one-half of these, 4,750,000, are male youth, the whole mass of whom wear ties, three-fourth's of them, 3,562,500. "snap" ties. One of these studs can be sold to at least one-fourth of this last number, which makes 890,625, on which the owner's profit, at five cents apiece, amounts to $44,531.25, and as the average life of a stud is about two years, this sum must be multiplied by eight to give whole profit for the seventeen years duration of the patent, which gives the comfortable product of $356,250.

THE CAPITAL REQUIRED is very small, and can be rapidly turned over.

FOR TERMS, ETC., address

GILES GENIUS.
Hartford, Conn.

This circular should be printed in good taste. If the inventor can afford to put it on heavy, tinted paper, in some fashionable type, as is the so called "old style" at present, with a red line around the edge for a border, so much the better. The matter of the circular should be written in as clear, crisp and sparkling style as the nature of the subject will admit, and the composition and press work be as perfect as possible.

If the inventor, himself, is not capable of doing justice to the subject, let him find some literary friend, or some other properly educated person, to do it for him. Let the statements be just as strong as the facts will bear. It will be observed that the terms are not given in this circular. This, with some other matters, can better be reserved for a written letter, to accompany the circular. It is advisable to accompany this circular with a written letter, for the reason that the receiver thereof will be obliged, in common courtesy, to give the matter attention enough to understand it, which attention he might not give to a mere circular. Besides, the letter makes the matter more of a personal thing to the receiver, and does not make the terms public, all of which tends to give weight to the matter. The general style may be understood from the following form for such a

(LETTER.)

[Confidential.]

HARTFORD, Conn., Jan. 1, 1871.

Mr. HIRAM HAUTBOY :

Dear Sir :—May I ask your careful attention to the enclosed circular ? I believe that the facts set forth therein will show you that I offer for sale a really valuable invention. The figures, making every possible allowance, and then dividing this by a large fraction, show that there is a fortune in this little thing. But I am in no condition to undertake the introduction of the article.

In the first place, I have no means.

In the next place, I am a mechanic. and ignorant of business ways and business men.

You are in a business which will enable you to manufacture and introduce this stud readily.

I offer you the whole patent for $5,000. I shall be satisfied to take part cash, and part approved notes. If you do not care to purchase the whole patent, I may be willing to sell you a territorial or shop right, or allow you to manufacture on a royalty.

This offer is made to you alone.

The thing will not be offered to any one else, unless you refuse to buy, when I shall offer it to others in your business. Be kind enough to answer at once. If an answer is not received by me within seven (7) days from this date, this offer is from that date withdrawn.   Very Respectfully,

GILES GENIUS.

This circular and letter should be sent to the different parties mentioned in the list, sending to but one party at a time, and waiting till the expiration of the seven days or other set time, for an answer, before sending to another.

When an answer is received looking toward negotiation, if any definite terms are offered, the inventor should most carefully consider upon it, before rejecting, even if greatly under the price asked, remembering always that all that is made over and above the actual expenses incurred, is clear profit. If a shop right, territorial right, or royalty right is wanted, the suggestions in the foregoing pages, on fixing the value of such rights, will be found of assistance.

If it is thought that better terms can be obtained, it is best to inform the correspondent that the inventor is "greatly obliged for the kind offer made, and will take it into serious consideration," etc., etc. A rule which should be imperative in all business matters, comes into play here. Never be rude or peremptory in declining an offer, but always express yourself in the kindest and pleasantest terms of which you are master.

It is hardly possible that an inventor of any merit can run the gauntlet, in this manner, of all the manufacturers in the country, whose business is of a kind to naturally interest them in the invention, without finding a purchaser.

NEWSPAPER ADVERTISING.

Another method of getting an invention before the public, is through the medium of newspaper advertising. This is more expensive than the method just described, and is not, perhaps, advisable till that fails, though it may be often happily used in conjunction with it. If the inventor can afford it, it is well to have the invention illustrated and described in one or more of the scientific and mechanical publications of the day, of which the Scientific American, and American Artisan, of New York, and the Scientific Press, of San Francisco, are notable examples. Such illustration and description may sometimes, of itself, prove sufficient. If not, it may be followed up by ordinary advertising ; or, this illustration and description may be dispensed with, and the advertising confined to the regular advertising columns. In doing this, the advertisement should be inserted in the paper or papers which are designed to meet the eye of the class or classes of persons to whom the invention is of special interest. Any reliable advertising agent will be pleased, on request, to furnish, free of charge, a list of any required size, extending over the whole country, or any part thereof, which circulate among any special class of people, and the advertisement of the invention should be inserted in one or more such papers, as the judgment and means of the inventor may dictate. It is very much better to insert a small advertisement in a large number of papers, than to occupy a large space in a smaller number. The experience of old advertisers confirms this proportion. If the inventor is not skilled in writing advertisements, it will be best for him, if possible, to get some friend, or other properly skilled person, to write the advertisement for him, for it is no common accomplishment to be able to put into a small space, in an attractive and striking, and yet not vulgar manner, a notice of any thing, which shall say just enough to induce the reader to push further inquiries. Suppose the invention to be an improvement in the manufacture of coach varnish: an advertisement something like the following, would not be inappropriate :

A NEW COACH VARNISH, oughly tried and tested. Address   A most valuable patented improvement in Coach Varnish is offered for sale—thoroughly tried and tested. Address   T. W. COPAL, Huyshope, Conn.

This will occupy but few lines of space, and yet tells enough to interest varnish and coach men therein. It is not advisable to make much parade of the patent, *as a patent*, for there is something of a prejudice among business men generally, against patents, on account of the great number of humbugs which have been pushed into notice under their guise, but this prejudice vanishes, when they discover that the patent covers a real improvement.

The proper papers in which to insert an advertisement like the above, would be those which are intended for circulation among varnish users, varnish manufacturers and carriage builders, a list of which, with the charge for insertion, the advertising agents can readily furnish. When answers to advertisements are received, they can be replied to by such a circular as that hereinbefore described, accompanied by a letter substantially like that set forth, changed to meet the requirements of the case.

The inventor must not be afraid, if his means permit, to continue his advertising for some little time, for experience has shown that unless a person is more than ordinarily interested in the matter advertised, he has to see an advertisement a number of times before he will take any active step in reference to it.

PERSONAL SOLICITATION.

Patents are frequently sold by personal solicitation, and if the inventor cares to make the sale of rights under his patent his main business, and can get safely through the period of rawness which always attends the commencement stage of all such attempts without giving up the business in disgust, this method of sale may prove, in the end, the most remunerative. The inventor must, however, give his whole time to the business, must have means sufficient to allow him to travel, and must persevere till he learns not to be discouraged at any and all disheartening obstacles he may encounter.

In short, he must make of himself a successful salesman, and a salesman of rather a rare order, a task which is evidently so difficult, that unless an inventor is satisfied he has peculiar qualifications for it, he better not undertake it. If he does, however,

see fit to undertake it, a few suggestions may be of assistance.
Upon arriving at a town where he proposes to make a sale, he
should be provided with a good model or models, and plenty of circulars containing substantially the matter set forth in the circular
hereinbefore described, making the closing part to read—" Rigbts
for sale on the most liberal terms at" (wherever the inventor has his
head-quarters). If the place boasts a newspaper, the matter should
be duly advertised, and good " local" notice will be found a great
help.

Suppose the invention to be a new domestic article, as a knife
sharpener, the advertisement might be in substance as follows :

" A GREAT WANT FILLED.—A simple, cheap and effective article for
use in every household. Great Profits made. Rights under the patent for sale
low. Call at —— ——   HARVEY HANDY, Patentee.

Of course, having interested a man enough to call, the
inventor must press upon him by aid of model, facts and figures,
etc., the money there is in it for the purchaser. If any resident of
the right stamp can be made to assist, by giving him a commission
on sales, it will prove a valuable help.

A thing sometimes done by traveling salesmen of patents is,
to find some resident who is " up to snuff," as the saying is, and
arrange with him that he shall hold himself out as ready to buy a
half interest in the territory which it is proposed to sell, and they
two, the salesman and the decoy duck, go in search of some third
party who will really buy the other half. The price of the territory
is put at double that which the seller really means to realize, and
when the third party is found to really buy the other half of the
right, the territory is assigned to the decoy duck and such party
jointly, but no money is paid, except by the third party, and out of
this the seller usually pays a commission to the decoy duck.

The fact that a neighbor is ready to purchase a half interest
in the right, is a great inducement, usually, to the third party to
buy the other half.

28

Of the morality of such transactions the reader will judge. If the inventor chooses to take his model in his hand, and attack parties most likely to become interested, at their places of business, he may make sales, but in this case he will find that previous advertising will pave the way for the personal effort.

ITINERANT AGENTS.

In almost every county in the United States may be found persons who, off and on, as the phrase is, make it their business to sell patent rights, traveling about the while for that purpose. It must, in truth, be said that some of these, by their fraudulent practices, have done much toward bringing the business of a traveling salesman of patents into disrepute. These fraudulent practices have consisted in making grossly false representations, as to the first cost of their articles, in taking notes for the whole or part of the consideration of the sales, under the promise to retain them till due, so that the purchaser should have a chance to see that their representations were true, before making final payment, and then selling the notes instanter, and the like.

Many of these men, the honest ones, are really good agents to employ, as they are usually willing to bear their own expenses, and take a share of the proceeds of the sales for their pay. If an inventor has a choice among different ones, he should, other things being equal, select the one who has means that make him pecuniarily responsible.

Unless a person has such means, or unless the inventor is satisfied that he is a man of the firmest integrity, it cannot be considered safe to give him an unlimited power of attorney to make sales, nor even then is it desirable, because it is always best to make sure that the agent cannot keep from the inventor any of the funds he may receive, nor put the patent into the hands of a confederate, by means of a bogus sale.

Control over the funds received can be kept, by providing, in the power of attorney, that all cash received shall be deposited to the joint order of the agent and the inventor, and that all notes taken shall be to their joint order.

Control over unadvisable or fraudulent sales can be kept by providing, in the power, that the sales made are conclusive, unless the inventor shall, within—say ten—days, signify his non-acceptance thereof. Forms for powers of attorney, with these or equivalent provisions, will be found further on.

STOCK COMPANIES.

A great many patents upon inventions which are either considered very valuable, or which require a large capital, to make them available, are realized from by making them the property of stock companies, which are either specially chartered by the state or national legislature, or are organized under the joint stock laws which prevail in most, if not all the states. This a perfectly legitimate, and often a very easy way of realizing money from an invention.

The inventor takes his pay either wholly in cash, or from stock in the company, or partly in cash and partly in stock.

The *modus operandi* is as follows :—the inventor, let us say, wishes to realize $10,000 in cash, and $10,000 in stock, and it is necessary to have $15,000 actual cash capital to work the patent.

\

In such a case the nominal capital of the company may, generally, well be put at $100,000.

We will, first of all, reserve $15,000 of this nominal capital to be used in securing the aid and countenance of influential men, to be given away by the inventor for this purpose, though of course this part of the operation is usually confidential between the inventor and those whose aid he seeks. The inventor must therefore reserve for himself, in all $25,000 of the nominal stock.

This leaves $75,000 in stock to be sold, whereby to realize $25,000 in cash, $10,000 for the inventor and $15,000 for actual cash capital.

Now, to raise $25,000 cash upon $75,000 nominal capital, each share sold needs to pay but one third of its nominal value, so that there is a great inducement in this for parties to invest in the stock.

Of course to make this operation successful, the inventor must be able to show, by facts and figures, a good prospect of paying from six to ten per cent dividends upon the nominal capital, and if he is able to do this, and acts with a fair amount of shrewdness in securing the help of two or three influential men, by the aid of the $15,000 in stock which he has set aside for this purpose, his task is very easy.

The inducements he may hold out to investors are not only the hope of gain from dividends, but the prospect of becoming officers of the company, as president, secretary, treasurer, director, etc. When such companies are organized, it is very common for the company to retain the services of the inventor in some capacity, so that the inventor is well rewarded by present cash, by stock, and by future employment.

If the inventor is content to take his pay entirely in stock, then his task is just so much the easier, and if he is able to organize his company without giving away stock, this again lightens his burden.

If the inventor is willing to put in his invention against, say, $10,000 actual cash capital, then he may be able to find two or three men, or possibly one man, who will put the cash against the invention ; and, in short, there are numberless ways in which this programme may be varied to meet the circumstances of each particular case.

The details of the organization of such companies must, of course, be performed under the direction of some competent lawyer, who will see that the local laws governing such matters are duly complied with, but farther on, in the part of this book devoted to forms, and instructions relative thereto, will be found a form for articles of association of this kind, such as is in use under the laws of the State of Connecticut, which laws are substantially the same as those of other states upon the same subject.

HOW TO WORK A SPECIALTY.

The following article, taken from the "Chemist and Druggist," published in London, although specially applicable to the sale of patent medicines, will be found very suggestive to all those who have patented articles to introduce :

"Without having the pretension to disclose any new systems, the writer will rapidly note a few of the various methods of establishing and developing the sale of proprietary articles, which have come under his personal observation, during a somewhat extended experience in England, France and America. Patent medicines, perfumeries, toilet preparations, dietetic productions, and other specialties are now so numerous, and in many instances are pushed so vigorously and with so much skill, that when it is proposed to launch any new item, or develop the sale of one already partially established, the magnitude of the task appears startling. To attract attention to any preparation, however good and well adapted to the wants of the public, is a task of such an expensive and laborious character, that a brief study of the systems followed by the successful men of the day, in this field, may be regarded as a topic of general interest. Whatever may be the scientific opinion in regard to the leading proprietary remedies in vogue, and however much their authors and compounders may lack professional status and a legitimate endorsement of their preparations, it is quite evident that hundreds of these men have succeeded in attracting public notice to themselves personally, as well as acquiring a great celebrity for their articles, by the unusual enterprise, skill, and general business talent displayed in the management of their specialties. It is not difficult to regard such men as likely to achieve success in almost any matter they may undertake, endowed, as they generally are, with the personal characteristics which emphatically command success. Therefore, it is quite correct to suppose that the great fortunes we hear of being accumulated by noted proprietors of specialties, are not exactly happy accidents, but the result of patient and intelligent labors, united to a judicious audacity and liberality.

"The personal acquaintance of the writer with a number of such men of the three nationalities already named, will enable him to indicate a few of the salient points in their methods of management. While it is quite true that many articles of questionable merit have, by mere force of publicity, been established on a remunerative sale, it is without any doubt essential to the success of preparations in general, that they should possess positive merit, and be well adapted to meet some general public want, otherwise the efforts made to introduce them will be full of difficulty. The notion sometimes heard—that advertising will make anything sell— is simple nonsense, as every large advertiser knows. Advertising will undoubtedly create a temporary demand for almost any article but unless the article itself responds to an evident public need, and is one which is intrinsically good, and likely to make its way on its own merits, as soon as the public attention to it has been gained, it will prove anything but a profitable enterprise, to make a serious campaign on such a basis.

"At this point, let a word be said on the utter inutility of investments in publicity, to develop sales of worthless and trivial articles ; and also let it be noted that all successful patent medicines, notwithstanding that they are oftentimes popularly denominated nostrums, quack remedies, &c., must, and often do possess intrinsic value, otherwise they could never attain any sale of magnitude or permanency. It is quite true that the enormous aggregate sales of patent medicines throughout the globe, a sale which has been extending with tremendous rapidity for the last decade, evidences a great popular want of cheap remedies which may be obtained in the shops, and which in many instances renders the expensive services of a medical man quite superfluous.

"The profession in France has legitimised patent remedies, and the popular verdict in other countries has been in their favor. In America, where, in consequence of the vastness of the territory, medical aid sometimes cannot be obtained for miles. these popular compounds are oftentimes of great service in maladies lacking gravity.

"In proceeding to notice more particularly the business aspects of the topic, it may be remarked that the introduction of a compound of undoubted excellence may be accomplished at a limited outgo, by adherence to certain very common sense methods too often lost sight of by enthusiastic projectors. The style of get-up of an article has oftentimes a considerable influence upon its success. The best illustrations are undoubtedly furnished by the French, who have, in the forms of their bottles, style of typography and wrapper, generally excelled the English and American productions.

"The retail prices should be in even shillings, francs, or dollars, although a contrary custom prevails in England and France ; and where various sizes of bottles are introduced, the prices should be the multiple each of the other, and the larger sizes contain relatively more than the smaller ones. The retail prices should always be printed upon the outside wrapper. The sending out of bottles of patent remedies without an outer wrapper is objectionable. The directions for use should always, no matter how voluminous they are, be wrapped around the bottle or box, inside of the wrapper ; it is decidedly objectionable to have them furnished separately, to be delivered by the retailers.

"The American plan of printing the title and other matter on the different sides of the bottle, in the four languages most in vogue, as well as full directions in all these languages, in the prospectus which is wrapped inside, is an excellent one. In the case of small toilet and remedial articles, the plan pursued in England of getting them up in counter cases is very effective for the purposes of introduction and advertisement, but too expensive to admit of after supplies being furnished in that way. The Americans have given a great deal of attention to putting dozens and half dozens in pasteboard boxes, with very bold outside labels. These, regularly arranged upon the shelves of a country druggist's shop, form a very cheap and effective advertisement, and also keep in good condition any bottles that may not be exposed for sale in the large plate glass counter show-cases so much in vogue there. For shipment, these paper boxes are packed generally in wooden cases of one dozen each, and these gross boxes are supplied without charge, the four sides being, when sent out by the proprietor, boldly branded with the title of the article. It is a common thing to notice in American druggists shops, piles of these wooden cases— many, no doubt, innocent of contents—but all forming very cheap and effective advertisements. The array of paper box "dummies" is also something wonderful, on the shelves and in the front windows, No box of this kind is ever destroyed, as long as there is any vacant space in the shop, its value in catching the eye of the customer being too great. These paper boxes and wooden cases are also well supplied with show bills, and small cards to hang up at odd corners of the shop, and a few dozen circulars for the counter, In some instances the gross cases contain beautifully gotten up illuminated show-cards, handsomely framed.

" From these details it will be perceived that the Americans are fully alive to the benefit to be derived from furnishing the retail dealer with a splendid supply of weapons for publicity in his shop. As the druggists there are much more willing to exhibit show bills and cards than the chemists in Europe, the rage for handsome ones has been carried to a most lavish point. Elaborately hand-painted gilt glass cards, three or four feet square, are quite common in the best shops, being furnished gratis by the leading patent medicine and perfumery makers, at a cost to themselves oftentimes of two or three guineas each.

" In deciding upon the retail price of an article about to be introduced, too much attention cannot be given to the discounts which will have to be made to the different classes of buyers in the trade. There should always be a first abatement from the retail trade of one-third, for any quantity to one who buys to sell again, and to the same party a further discount of, say, ten per cent, when a whole gross is purchased—this last to be supplemented by an additional discount of ten or fifteen per cent. to the wholesale houses on five or ten gross lots. As the class of goods in question is essentially a monopoly, the proprietor has power to fix his prices as arbitrarily as he chooses, but he will consult his interest by making liberal discounts, selling for net cash only, and in no case, confidentially or otherwise, giving any advantage to one buyer over another. A printed tariff to wholesale houses should he issued, and rigidly adhered to as to quantities, cash, and days allowed for payment. All changes in this tariff should be notified some considerable time in advance of the period when the change will take place, so as to give wholesale dealers time to arrange advantageously, in case of their being either over-stocked or in short supply. These notices should be given simultaneously, that no one man may have any advantrge from early information of contemplated changes. Having experienced the desirability of this uniformity of dealing with the trade in specialties, the writer is disposed to lay great stress upon it. The proprietor of an article must obviously, in arranging his wholesale and retail prices, allow himself a handsome margin, the expense for publicity and otherwise, aside from the cost of manufacture, being likely to be so onerous. If, as is often the case, an article is got up by a chemist, in the midst of the ordinary routine of his shop, without adding anything for expense of labor, he should not, on that account, omit to include in his estimate the probable cost of bottling, packing, etc., as in all articles of extended sale, a separate organization and force becomes essential. The probable fluctuations in the ingredients of which the preparation is composed, should also be carefully taken into account, as the variation of a price once fixed upon a proprietary article is likely to be damaging. The heavy war tax upon spirits in the United States, a few years ago, (now reduced,) nearly ruined the smaller grade of patent medicine men there, and they were obliged to adopt prices in many cases fifty and one hundred per cent. higher, which resulted in placing their preparations quite out of the reach of men of moderate means. Coming to the actual work of introducing an article, it is better for persons of moderate means to canvas in the outset large country towns, than to attack the great cities. Should abundant means be at command, the metropolis had better be taken in hand first, as the country naturally sympathises in the demand for a preparation which has a metropolitan vogue, even where no local expenditure is made for publicity.

"Whatever field is taken up in the outset, it should be thoroughly worked, and the article well made known there, before wasting time and scattering efforts in other quarters. No more common mistake is made by sanguine projectors of specialties than in endeavoring to grasp the whole body of the people at once. Any advertisement contracts made should be for cash, or nearly so. It is so easy to get out of one's depth in making contracts payable out of prospective profits. When an article is already launched, and has been favorably received, the extension of its advertisements with a certain amount of boldness is no longer so pure a risk.

"The question of newspaper advertising is so broad a one, that the limits of this article will hardly suffice for its treatment. Briefly, it must be quite clear that all feeble, cheap advertising, in the obscure columns of the papers, has but little effect. The shrewdest advertisers of the day adopt the most expensive methods, choosing the most costly localities in the principal journals. A few lines at several shillings a line, in a prominent part of a newspaper is a better investment than a lengthy advertisement in an obscure column at half the expense. Continuous advertising in every issue of a daily or weekly newspaper, is a great waste of money. If six advertisements on six successive days lead to an expenditure of ten pounds, it would be much more effective to insert one advertisement once a week at an expense of half the money. Small announcements persisted in, if appearing continuously, will undoubtedly, in time, produce a favorable result ; but, for immediate sales, resort must be had to bold, and sometimes to lengthy announcements. A dignified phraseology should always be adhered to, but any novelty that can be secured in point of typographical display, is eminently desirable,

" It is very questionable if the paragraph notices of a facetious character, now somewhat in favor with advertisers in the leading dailies, are really effective. The locality chosen is the advantage, if there is one ; but, obviously, the notion that the public are supposing they are absorbing the regular reading matter of the newspaper, is presuming too much on their credulity. Of all forms of advertising, none approaches the well established daily newspaper. Where there are several published in one town, it is better, in default of ability to grasp them all, to choose the best one for the article in hand, and go in liberally. *Small advertising does not pay.*

"When an article is being introduced, there should always be affixed to all advertisements the name of one or two shops in the town where it is kept on sale. This saves much disappointment on the part of intending buyers, who often apply at a dozen places without success, and ultimately give up their idea of obtaining it. "For sale by all chemists," is a very bad line to add to an advertisement of a new article. Nine out of every ten dealers will say, "We never heard of it before," and the tenth one will offer to procure it ; while all (if in America) will suggest that "It's a new thing," "Don't know much about it yet," "We have something of our own of the same kind quite as good." All of these influences have to be fought against by the projector of something new, and even at the risk of making some shops jealous, it is much better to name one or two where the article can surely be obtained.

"Nothing is so successful as success. Once an article is well established, the chorus is unanimous in its favor from all the shop-keepers ; during its struggling infancy, something seems to whisper to them to give it a kick.

"Previous to quitting the party "who never heard of it before," it may be well to direct his attention to the eminently modern plan of *advertising to the trade,* now so much in favor with the most intelligent body of advertisers. The last few years have witnessed the establishment of a most excellent series of class and trade journals in several countries—more especially in England —addressing themselves to readers of various professions and kinds of business. To all projectors of new specialties, this class of journals is invaluable, as well as to the proprietors of such established ones as it is desirable to keep alive in the minds of the trade. A great step in advance is made, if the trade can at once be thoroughly informed respecting a new article. In default of ability to inaugurate an extensive range of advertising to the public, a most important impression can be made by bold announcements in suitable class journals ; and in conjunction with an elaborate programme of publicity, the columns of this branch of the press offer palpable advantages. These journals, although as yet in a successful infancy, are destined to occupy a greatly enlarged position and influence. The day is rapidly approaching, in fact has arrived, when the intelligent chemist must regularly peruse a periodical specially edited and published for himself and his confreres, in order to keep up with the advances made in the scientific branches of his profession, as well as to be thoroughly posted in its special trade intelligence. Obviously, these are among the earliest channels in which originators of specialties should communicate with the trade, beginning by at once making their articles known, by name at least, to the whole body."

FORMS AND INSTRUCTIONS

FOR

Assignments, Grants, Licenses,

CONTRACTS, ETC.

ASSIGNMENTS AND GRANTS.

An Assignment of a patent right is an instrument in writing, conveying either the whole interest in the patent, or an undivided part thereof.

A Grant is an instrument in writing, conveying an exclusive territorial right under a patent.

The following is the text of the law with reference thereto, Approved July 8, 1870.

" Section 36. *And be it further enacted,* That every patent, or any interest therein, shall be assignable in law, by an instrument in writing, and the patentee, or his assign, or legal representative, may, in like manner, grant and convey an exclusive right, under his patent, to the whole or any specified part of the United States, and said assignment and grant, or conveyance, shall be void, as against any subsequent purchaser or mortgagee for a valuable consideration, without notice, unless it be recorded in the Patent Office within three months from the date thereof."

The following quoted paragraphs are from the Patent Office " Rules ;"

" A patent may be assigned, either as to the whole interest, or any undivided part thereof, by any instrument of writing. No particular form of words is necessary to constitute a valid assignment, nor need the instrument be sealed, witnessed, or acknowledged."

" A patent will, upon request, issue directly to the assignee or assignees of the entire interest in any invention, or to the inventor and the assignee jointly, when an undivided part only of the entire interest has been conveyed."

" In every case where a patent issues or reissues to an assignee, the assignment must be recorded at the Patent Office at least five days before the issue of the Patent, and the specification must be sworn to by the inventor."

"The patentee may grant and convey an exclusive right under his patent, to the whole or any specified portion of the United States, by an instrument in writing."

"Every assignment or grant of an exclusive territorial right must be recorded in the Patent Office, within three months from the execution thereof; otherwise it will be void as against any subsequent purchaser or mortgagee for a valuable consideration without notice ; but, if recorded after that time, it will protect the assignee or grantee against any such subsequent purchaser, whose assignment or grant is not then on record."

"The patentee may convey separate rights under his patent to make, or to use, or to sell his invention, or he may convey territorial or shop rights which are not exclusive. Such conveyances are mere licenses, and need not be recorded."

" The receipt of assignments is not generally acknowledged by the office. They will be recorded in their turn within a few days after their reception, and then transmitted to the persons entitled to them. A five cent revenue stamp is required for each sheet or piece of paper on which an assignment, grant, or license may be written."

The fees for recording assignments, grants, contracts, or any other paper which should be forwarded, with the papers for record, to the " Com'r of Patents, Washington, D. C." are as follows :

For recording an instrument of 100 words or under................$1.00
" " " over 300 and under 1000 words.2.00
" " " over 1000 words...................3.00

In sending papers to the Patent Office for record, the papers and the money should be acompanied by a letter, stating that the enclosed papers are for record, and that the enclosed money is the fee for the same, and stating the address to which the papers are to be returned.

45

FORMS.

NO. 1. ASSIGNMENT OF THE ENTIRE INTEREST, BEFORE THE ISSUE OF THE PATENT, (BY SOLE INVENTOR.)

In consideration of *one dollar*, to me paid by *John J. Smith*, of *Hartford, Conn.*, I do hereby sell and assign to said *John J. Smith*, all my right, title and interest in and to a certain invention in *plows*, as fully set forth and described in the specification which I have prepared, (if the application has been made, say "and filed,") preparatory to obtaining letters patent of the United States therefor, and I do hereby authorize and request the Commissioner of Patents to issue the said letters patent to my said assignee, for the sole use and behoof of said assignee, and his legal representatives.

Witness my hand this 1*st* day of *June*, 1871.

CHARLES CHANDLER.

The words and figures in italics denote those which are to be changed to suit different cases, and the same is true of all the following forms in the book, except that where changes are to be made from the singular to the plural, or *vice versa*, italics will not be used.

NO. 2. ASSIGNMENT OF AN UNDIVIDED INTEREST, BEFORE ISSUE OF PATENT, (BY JOINT INVENTORS.)

In consideration of *one dollar*, to us paid by *John J. Smith*, of *Hartford, Conn.*, we do hereby sell and assign to him *one undivided half* interest in and to a certain invention in *plows*, as fully set forth and described in the specification which we have prepared, (if application has been made say, "and filed,") preparatory to obtaining letters patent of the United States therefor. And we do hereby authorize and request the Commissioner of Patents to issue said letters patent to said assignee and ourselves jointly, for the sole use

46

and behoof of said assignee and ourselves, and his and our legal representatives.

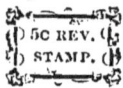

Witness our hands this 2d day of *June*, 1871.

CHARLES CHANDLER,
DARIUS DOMBEY.

NO. 3. ASSIGNMENT OF ENTIRE (OR UNDIVIDED PARTIAL) INTEREST, AFTER ISSUE OF PATENT, (BY SOLE INVENTOR.)

In consideration of *five hundred dollars*, to me paid by *John J. Smith*, of *Hartford Conn.*, I do hereby assign and sell to said *John J. Smith*, all my right, title and interest, (or *one* undivided *half* interest) in and to the letters patent of the United States, No. 41,806, for an improvement in *plows*, granted to me *July* 30, 1864, the same to be held and enjoyed by my said assignee to the full end of the term for which said patent is granted, as fully and entirely as the same would have been held and enjoyed by me, if this assignment had not been made.

Witness my hand this 10th day of *June*, 1871.

CHARLES CHANDLER.

NO. 4. ASSIGNMENT OF AN ENTIRE (OR UNDIVIDED) INTEREST IN PATENT AND EXTENSION THEREOF, (BY SOLE INVENTOR.)

In consideration of *one thousand* dollars to me paid by *John J. Smith*, of *Hartford, Conn.*, I do hereby sell and assign to the said *John J. Smith*, all my right title and interest (or an undivided *half* interest) in and to the letters patent of the United States, No. 10,485, for an improvement in *plows*, granted to me *May* 16, 1865, the same to be held and enjoyed by the said *John J. Smith*, to the full end of the term for which said letters patent are granted, and for the term of any extension thereof, as fully and entirely as the samo would have been held and enjoyed by me, if this assignment had not been made.

Witness my hand this 4*th* day of *January*, 1871.

50 REV. STAMP.

CHARLES CHANDLER.

The clause with reference to extension can have no force, except with those patents granted prior to March 2, 1861, unless the law shall be changed hereafter, which is very unlikely, or unless extended by special act of Congress.

UNDIVIDED INTERESTS.

It is very important that all persons interested in patents should understand that the owner of an undivided interest in a patent, no matter how small, may, if he choose, carry on the manufacture and sale of the patented article to any extent, without any liability to account therefor to the owner or owners of the remainder of the patent; he may; also, grant all the licenses he pleases, and put all the money he gets therefor into his pocket, and keep it there, so that, unless the assignor desire just this state of things, a proper limiting clause, in the nature of a condition, putting it beyond the power of the assignee, or assignor, so to do, should be put into the assignment. Although the writer has not, in considerable practice as patent attorney, come upon an assignment drawn by any one else, which contained such a condition, he has never found an assignor who did not insist on having it, when the matter was explained to him. The next form, which is otherwise the same in substance as its immediate predecessor, No. 4, contains such a condition, printed in small capitals, which can readily be inserted in the same place in all the other forms.

48

No. 5. SAME AS NO 4, WITH CONDITION.

In consideration of *one thousand dollars* to me paid by *John J. Smith*, of *Hartford, Conn.*, I do hereby sell and assign to the said *John J. Smith*, one undivided *half* interest in and to the letters patent of the United States, No. 10,485, for an improvement in *plows*, granted to me *May 16*, *1865*, the same to be held and enjoyed by the said *John J. Smith* to the full end of the term for which said letters patent are granted, and for the term of any extension thereof.

THIS ASSIGNMENT IS MADE UPON THE FOLLOWING EXPRESS CONDITION, WHICH FORMS AN INTEGRAL PART OF THE SAME, TO WHICH SAID CONDITION THE ASSIGNOR ASSENTS BY THE ACT OF SIGNING THIS INSTRUMENT, AND TO WHICH THE ASSIGNEE ASSENTS BY THE ACT OF ACCEPTING THE SAME, OR DOING ANY ACT UNDER AND BY VIRTUE OF ITS AUTHORITY, TO WIT :—NEITHER THE ASSIGNOR NOR THE ASSIGNEE MENTIONED HEREIN HAVE ANY RIGHT, POWER OR LIBERTY TO MAKE, OR VEND TO OTHERS TO BE USED, THE ARTICLE (OR " PROCESS," " MACHINE," " COMPOUND," WHATEVER IT MAY BE) WHICH FORMS THE -SUBJECT MATTER OF SAID PATENT, WITHOUT THAT HE SHALL ACCOUNT AND PAY OVER TO THE OTHER PARTY HERETO ONE HALF OF ALL THE PROFIT DERIVED FROM SUCH MAKING, USING, OR VENDING TO OTHERS TO BE USED, NOR SHALL EITHER OF SAID PARTIES HERETO HAVE ANY POWER TO MAKE ANY ASSIGNMENT, GRANT, LICENSE OR OTHER CONVEYANCE WHATEVER HEREUNDER, EXCEPT THAT BOTH OF SAID PARTIES SHALL JOIN IN THE SAME IN WRITING.

Witness my hand this 10*th* day of *June*, 1871.

CHARLES CHANDLER.

No. 6. GRANT OF EXCLUSIVE TERRITORIAL RIGHT, (BY ASSIGNEES.)

In consideration of *one thousand* dollars to us paid by *Wm. H. Dinsmore* and *James S. Sanborn*, of *Concord, New Hampshire*, we do hereby assign, grant and convey to the said *Wm. H. Dins-*

more and *James S. Sanborn*, the exclusive right to make, use and vend within the *State* of *Wisconsin*, and in no other place or places, the improvement in *plows*, for which letters patent of the United States, dated *August 25*, 1867, were granted to *Lemuel H. Harvey*, and by said *Harvey* duly assigned to us, and recorded in the Patent Office, the same to be held and enjoyed by the said *William H. Dinsmore* and *James S. Sanborn*, as full and entirely as the same would have been held and enjoyed by us, if this grant had not been made.

Witness our hands this 19*th* day of *June*, 1871.

CHARLES CHANDLER,
HENRY H. HARRIS.

It is believed that a careful reading of the above forms will enable any fairly intelligent person to draw an assignment or grant to meet any particular case, taking the phraseology wholly from one form, or partly from one and partly from another, as the circumstances in hand dictate.

LICENSES.

A license under a patent is an oral or written permit to make, sell, or use a patented invention, conveying no interest in the patent itself, and it need not be recorded.

A license may be made by the owner of the entire, or an undivided interest in a patent, or by the owner of an exclusive territorial right. An owner of a license, which, by its terms, is assignable, can assign it to other parties at his pleasure. Licenses require a five cent revenue stamp upon each sheet or piece of paper upon which they are written. The following are forms of license:

No. 1. LICENSE—SHOP RIGHT, (BY PATENTEE.)

In consideration of *fifty* dollars paid me by *Hart, Holbrook, & Company*, of *Albany, New York*, I do hereby license and em-

50

power said firm to manufacture at *a single foundry and machine shop* in said *Albany*, and in no other place or places, the improvement in *harrows*, for which letters patent of the United States *No.* 71,846 were granted to me *November* 13, 1868, and to sell the machines so manufactured throughout the United States, to the full end of the term for which said letters patent are granted.

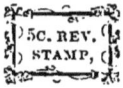

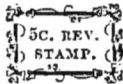

Witness my hand this 22d day of *June*, 1871.

NOEL HOLCOMB.

NO. 2. LICENSE—SHOP RIGHT—ASSIGNABLE AND LIMITED, (BY PATENTEES.)

In consideration of *fifty dollars*, we do hereby license *Hiram A. Evarts*, of *Kingston*, *New York*, or his assigns, to manufacture at a single foundry and machine shop, the improved *seed sower*, for which letters patent of the United States *No.* 74,560 were granted to us *December* 15, 1870, to the number of *one hundred* of such *seed sowers* in each calendar year, and no more, and to sell such *seed sowers* so made in the United States, to the full end of the term for which said letters patent are granted.

Witness our hands this 24th day of *June*, 1871.

HARLOW HUGGINS,
JAMES E. JILLSON.

NO. 3. LICENSE—NOT EXCLUSIVE—WITH CONTRACT FOR ROYALTY.
(Taken from Patent Office Forms.)

This agreement, made the 12th day of *September*, 1868, between *Morrison White*, party of the first part, and *the Uniontown Agricultural Works*, party of the second part, witnesseth that whereas letters patent of the United States for an improvement in *horse rakes* were granted to the party of the first part, dated *October* 4, 1867 ; and whereas the party of the second part is desirous of manufacturing *horse rakes* containing said patented improvement ; now, therefore, the parties have agreed as follows :

İ. The party of the first part hereby licenses and empowers the party of the second part to manufacture, subject to the conditions hereinafter named, at *their factory in Uniontown, Maryland*, and in no other place or places, to the end of the term for which said letters patent were granted, *horse rakes* containing the patented improvements, and to sell the same within the United States.

II. The party of the second part agrees to make full and true returns to the party of the first part, under oath, upon the first days of July and January in each year, of all *horse rakes* containing the patented improvements manufactured by them.

III. The party of the second part agrees to pay to the party of the first part *five dollars*, as a license fee upon every *horse rake* manufactured by said party of the second part, containing the patented improvements ; provided that, if the said fee be paid upon the days provided herein for semi-annual returns, or within ten days thereafter, a discount of fifty per cent. shall be made from said fee for prompt payment.

IV. Upon failure of the party of the second part to make returns, or to make payment of license fees, as herein provided, for thirty days after the days herein named, the party of the first part may terminate this license by serving a written notice upon the party of the second part ; but the party of the second part shall not thereby be discharged from any liability to the party of the first part, for any license fees due at the time of the service of said notice.

In witness whereof, the parties above named (*the said Uniontown Agricultural Works, by its president*) have hereunto set their hands this day and year first above written.

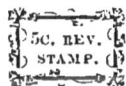

MORRISON WHITE.
UNIONTOWN AGRICULTURAL WORKS,
By JABEZ REYNOLDS, *President.*

No. 4. LICENSE—EXCLUSIVE—WITH CONTRACT FOR ROYALTY.

This agreement, made this 10th day of *June*, 1871, between *Henry L. Harrison*, of *Hartford*, *Connecticut*, party of the first part, and *the Excelsior Iron Works*, *a corporate body under the laws of said state, located and doing business at New Britain, in said state*, party of the second part, witnesseth—

That whereas letters patent of the United States were, on the 29th day of *January*, 1871, granted to said party of the first part, for an improvement in *stove hooks*, which said patented article said party of the second part is desirous to make and sell ; now, therefore, the parties have agreed as follows :

I. The party of the first part hereby gives to the party of the second part, the exclusive right to manufacture and sell said patented improvements, to the end of the term of said patent, subject to the conditions hereinafter named.

II. The party of the second part agrees to make full and true returns, on the first days of January, April, July and October in each year, of all of said patented *stove hooks* made by them in the three calendar months then last past, and if said party of the first part shall not be satisfied, in any respect, with any such return, then he shall have the right, either by himself or his attorney, to examine any and all of the books of account of said party of the second part, containing any items, charges, memoranda or information relating to the manufacture or sale of said patented *stove hooks*, and upon request made, said party of the second part shall produce all such books for said examination.

III. The party of the second part agree to pay the party of the first part *two cents* as a license fee upon every one of said patented *stove hooks* made by them, the whole of said license fee for each quarterly term of three months, as hereinbefore specified to be due and payable within *fifteen days* after the regular return day for that quarter. And said party of the second part agrees to pay to the party of the first part at least *fifty dollars*, as said license fee, upon each of said quarterly terms, even though they should not make enough of said patented *stove hooks* to amount to that sum at the regular royalty of *two cents* apiece.

IV. Upon failure of the party of the second part to make returns, or to make payment of license fees as herein provided, for *thirty* days after such returns or such payments are due respectively, then the party of the first part may terminate this license by serving a written notice to that effect upon the party of the second part; but said party of the second part shall not thereby be discharged from any liability to the party of the first part for any license fees due at the time of the service of said notice.

In witness whereof the above named parties (*the said Excelsior Iron Works, by its President*) have hereto set their hands this day and year first above written.

5C. REV. STAMP.

   HENRY L. HARRISON,
    Excelsior Iron Works,
  By JOHN HARTSHORN, President.

It will be observed that under form No. 3, the licensee is not bound to make a single one of the patented articles, and if he does not, the patentee derives no profit from the license. It is not an uncommon thing for unscrupulous manufacturers, with whose business a new invention would interfere, to get a license in substance like form No. 3, except to make it exclusive, and perhaps leave out the vacating clause at the end, and then to either never make a single one of the patented articles, or to make so few as to make it really amount to the same thing. The license in form No. 4 is the one that is recommended, for under it the licensee is bound to pay a certain sum, as royalty, whether he make a single one of the articles or not.

No. 5. TRANSFER OF TRADE MARK.

(From Patent Office Forms.)

We, Jotham Mills and Abner Clark, of *Keokuk, Iowa, partners under the firm name of Mills & Clark,* in consideration of *five hundred dollars,* to us paid by *Jarvis Case,* of *the same place,* do hereby sell, assign, and transfer to the said *Jarvis Case* and his assigns the exclusive right to use, in the manufacture of *stoves,* a certain trade mark for *stoves,* deposited by us in the United States Patent Office, and recorded therein *July 15,* 1870; the same to be held, enjoyed and used by the said *Jarvis Case* as fully and entirely as the same would have been held and enjoyed by *us,* if this grant had not been made.

Witness our hands this *20th* day of *July,* 1870.

JOTHAM MILLS,
ABNER CLARK.

FORM FOR ARTICLES OF ASSOCIATION

(OF THE

WILLIAMS PATENT STEAM GOVERNOR
MANUFACTURING COMPANY.)

The subscribers hereby associate themselves as a body corporate and politic, under and in pursuance of the provisions of the statute laws of the State of *Connecticut,* authorizing and regulating the formation of joint stock corporations, and they adopt the following general articles of association and agreement:

I. The name of the corporation shall be the *Williams Patent Steam Governor Manufacturing Company,* and its capital stock shall be *one hundred thousand* dollars, to be divided into shares of twenty-five dollars each.

II. The purpose for which this said corporation is to be organized is *to manufacture and sell the steam governor covered by letters patent of the United States, dated February 29, 1871, and numbered 102,232, issued to Chauncey Williams, to sell rights under said letters patent*, and to buy and sell, and deal generally in such real and personal estate as may be necessary and convenient in the successful prosecution of said business.

III. The principal place of business of said corporation shall be at *Hartford*, in said state.

IV. Each subscriber hereto agrees to take the number of shares in the capital stock of said corporation set against his name, to be paid for by installments, as called for by the directors hereafter to be appointed.

V. It is mutually understood and agreed by and between the subscribers hereto, that said *Chauncey Williams*, or his legal representatives, may subscribe hereto for that number of shares, whose par value amounts to *twenty-five thousand* dollars, and that when said letters patent are fully assigned to said corporation, said *Williams*, and his legal representatives, shall be freed from any further liability on account thereof, which said allowance, together with *ten thousand* dollars in cash, which it is agreed and understood shall be paid to said *Williams* before said corporation shall commence to prosecute said business, shall be in full payment for said letters patent, and the invention covered thereby, which shall then become the full and exclusive property of said corporation.

Dated *Hartford, Conn., July 4th*, 1871.

NAMES.	NO. OF SHARES.	PAR VALUE.

Upon such a basis as this, the inventor can proceed, till he secures the requisite subscribers, after which it is advisable to follow the advice of some local attorney, as to giving notice of the first meeting of the company, etc.

FORMS

FOR

POWERS OF ATTORNEY

TO

SELL RIGHTS, ETC.

WITH

INSTRUCTIONS, ETC.

FORMS FOR POWER OF ATTORNEY.

NO. 1.   POWER, OF ATTORNEY.
(By the Patentee.)

I, *John Haight*, of *Hartford*, *Connecticut*, patentee and owner of letters patent of the United States, No. 100,001, for an improvement in *Mouse Traps*, dated *May* 10, 1870, do hereby appoint *Hiram Handsome*, of said *Hartford*, my attorney, with full power to make assignments, grants, or licenses of any kind, under said patent, with full power to sign my name to all such instruments, and to receive and receipt for all considerations received in exchange for any of said rights, but with no power to bind me in any manner further than to make binding and legal all such assignments, grants and licenses.

This power is in force till a revocation in writing shall be duly recorded upon the records of the United States Patent Office, where this power of attorney will be found duly recorded.

Witness my hand this 14*th* day of *June*, A. D. 1871.

JOHN HAIGHT.

Witnesses,
Charles H. Hauser,
Henry C. Cable.

50c.
REVENUE STAMP.

It will be observed that the foregoing power gives to the attorney, while the power is unrevoked, as full power over the patent as the owner has, and makes no provision for ensuring that the owner shall know of the terms of each sale, or for the safety of the funds received. Although it is a common form, it cannot be recommended. The following is the form that is recommended :

No. 2. POWER OF ATTORNEY, (WITH RESTRICTIONS.)

(By the Assignees of entire right.)

We, *William M. Noble* and *Hugh R. Ransom*, of *Hartford, Connecticut*, assignees and owners of the entire right in and to letters patent of the United States No. 100,002, for an improvement in *Garden Hoes*, dated *May* 10, 1870, do hereby appoint *Harvey Handy*, of said *Hartford*, our attorney, with full power to make assignments, grants or licenses of any kind, under said patent, with full power to sign our names to all such instruments, and to receive and receipt for, in our name, all considerations received in exchange for any of said rights, but with no power to bind us, or either of us, further than to make binding and legal all such assignments, grants, and licenses, he to exercise all power herein conferred under the following conditions, without which no act of his under this authority shall be valid.

I. He shall sell at not less than the following prices :

For the whole patent, $20,000.

For any state, such part of $20,000 as the population of the state in question bears ratio to the whole population of the United States, this result to be doubled to find the price for said state.

For any county, such part of the price for the state, as determined by the foregoing directions, as the population of the said county bears ratio to the population of the state, this result to be doubled to find the value of said county.

For any town, such part of the price of the county in which it is situated, determined as hereinbefore directed, as the population of the town bears ratio to the population of the county, this result to be doubled to find the value of said town.

All sales of licenses, and all territorial sales at less than the prices given above, to be subject to our approval by letter or telegram.

II. All payments for rights thus sold shall be made either in cash wholly, or in not less than one half cash, and one half in good promissory notes, to mature within six months from day of sale, and either signed or endorsed by a person or persons of ample pecuniary responsibility. All such cash shall be deposited by the payer thereof with the nearest bank, or responsible private banker, payable to the joint order of our said attorney and ourselves, and all such promissory notes shall be made in three notes of equal amount, payable to the joint order of ourselves and our said attorney, and delivered to him. Any payment aforesaid in anywise deviating from these provisions, to be subject to our approval by letter or telegram.

This power shall remain in force till a written revocation thereof shall be recorded on the records of the Patent Office of the United States, where this power will be found recorded.

Witness our hands this 10th day of *June*, A. D. 1871.

Witnesses, *WILLIAM M. NOBLE*,
Samuel S. Simmons, *HUGH R. RANSOM.*
Thomas T. Tompkins.

```
50 CENT
REVENUE STAMP.
```

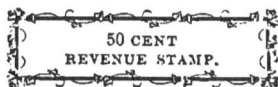

The reader is, probably, not artless enough to need the suggestion that it is well to put the stated price in the power high enough to allow the agent to fall sensibly therefrom, and yet get a fair price. There is nothing that will incite a person to buy an article so much as to think he is getting it much below its real value.

NO. 3. PRIVATE AGREEMENT TO ACCOMPANY POWER OF ATTORNEY.

This agreement made this 10th day of *June*, 1871, between *William M. Noble* and *Hugh R. Ransom*, party of the first part, and *Harvey Handy*, party of the second part, all of *Hartford, Ct.*, Witnesseth,

I. That the party of the second part agrees to use his best endeavors to sell rights under letters patent *No.* 100,002, dated *May* 10, 1871, for the party of the first part, under the terms and conditions of a power of attorney of even date herewith, from the party of the first part to the party of the second part, such endeavors to continue until said power of attorney is revoked, or until the party of the second part notifies the party of the first part, in writing, that he no longer wishes to be bound by this agreement.

II. The party of the first part agrees to pay to the party of the second part one third part of all the proceeds from said sales, as remuneration for his services in this behalf, and this remuneration shall be due and payable from cash received, as soon as deposited as provided in said power of attorney, and from promissory notes received, as soon as the same are delivered to the party of the second part, the party of the second part to retain as his property one of the three said equal promissory notes, and to immediately forward the other two to party of the first part. This allowance to be in full of all charges whatsoever, in this behalf, against party of the first part, and said party of the second part is to bear his own expenses, of whatever nature.

In witness whereof the said parties have hereto set their hands this 10*th* day of *June*, A. D. 1871.

Witnesses,   5C. REV. STAMP.   *WILLIAM M. NOBLE,*
Samuel S. Simmons,   *HUGH R. RANSOM,*
Thos. T. Tompkins.   *HARVEY HANDY.*

Both parties should have one of these agreements, which should be made in duplicate for that purpose; of course, this agreement is for nothing but private use, and is not to be shown generally.

63

No. 4. REVOCATION OF POWER OF ATTORNEY.

Having, on the 10*th* day of *June*, 1871, appointed *Harvey Handy*, of *Hartford, Conn.*, our attorney to sell rights under letters patent *No.* 100,002, dated *May* 10, 1871, for us, we do hereby, for full and sufficient reasons, revoke said power of attorney to him, and declare his authority to act for us in any manner to be at an end.

Witness our hands this 4*th* day of *July*, A. D. 1871, at *Hartford, Conn.*

Witnesses,   *WM. M. NOBLE,*

Sam. S. Simmons,   *HUGH R. RANSOM.*

Thos. T. Tompkins.

No. 5. POWER OF ATTORNEY TO SELL RIGHTS, C. O. D.

I, *Charles Cautious*, of *Hartford, Conn.*, owner of letters patent of the United States No. 102,204, dated *February 29th*, 1871, hereby authorize *Hiram Handy*, of said *Hartford*, to sell assignments, grants and licenses under said patent, such sales to be approved by me before becoming valid, upon which approval in each case, I will send the necessary assignment, grant or license, duly executed by me, by express to said *Handy*, accompanied with instructions to the carrier to allow said *Handy*, and the buyer or buyers of any such right, to examine such conveyance, and upon delivery of the same, to collect for return to me such money, notes, or articles as I am to receive in consideration of such sale.

Signed and sealed by me, this 31*st* day of *June*, A. D. 1871.

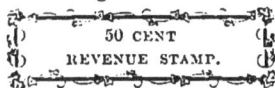

                     CHARLES CAUTIOUS,   L. S.

50 CENT REVENUE STAMP.

All powers of attorney to sell rights, and all revocations thereof, should be recorded at the Patent Office, so that buyers may have full notice of a revocation, and be protected thereagainst. Notwithstanding the provision in the power of attorney that the attorney shall only sell for cash and notes, it is well to agree verbally that he may sell for real estate, subject, of course, to approval by letter or telegram, and when this is done, the deed for the same can be made to the joint names of the owner, or owners, of the patent and the attorney, and the land can afterward be divided, if not satisfactorily sold for cash, allowing the attorney one-third, as in other cases. If articles of personal property, as produce, horses, diamonds, etc., are offered in exchange for rights, it is best to take them, and then sell them for cash.

MORTGAGE OF PATENTS.

Although the patent law does not expressly provide for mortgage of patents, it plainly indicates that such mortgages can be made, for the last part of section 36, Act of July 8, 1870, reads.

"— and said assignment, grant, or conveyance shall be void, as against any subsequent purchaser or *mortgagee*, for a valuable consideration," etc., etc.

This may sometimes avail as a security whereon to borrow money, and the following is a form :

NO. 1. FORM FOR MORTGAGE OF PATENT.

In consideration of *five hundred dollars*, to me paid by *Chauncey C. Colton*, of *Canton, Connecticut*, I do hereby assign and mortgage to said *Chauncey C. Colton*, all my right, title and interest in and to a certain invention in *rakes*, as fully set forth and described in letters patent of the United States No. 100.003, dated

January 29, 1871, of which invention and letters patent I am sole owner.

The condition of this assignment is such that whereas, I am justly indebted to said *Colton* in the sum of *five hundred* dollars, as evidenced by my promissory note of even date herewith, payable to said *Colton*, or order, *one year* from date, with interest; now, if said note shall be well and truly paid according to its tenor, then this assignment and mortgage shall be null and void; otherwise to be of full force and effect.

In witness whereof I hereto set my hand and seal this 10*th* day of *June*, 1871.

Witnesses, *ABRAM ANDERSON*, ⟦L. S.⟧

Barton B. Brown,
Charles C. Colter.

State of *Connecticut,*⟩ ss. *Hartford, June* 10*th*, 1871.
County of *Hartford,* ⟩

Then personally appeared before me, the subscribing authority, *Abram Anderson*, signer and sealer of the foregoing instrument, and acknowledged the same to be his free act and deed.

⟦SEAL OF COURT.⟧ ⟦50 CENT REVENUE STAMP.⟧

DARIUS D. DERBY,
Clerk of the Superior Court
for said County.

Since that an assignment of a patent needs not to be sealed, witnessed nor acknowledged, perhaps the same formalities can be dispensed with in a mortgage, but as such a mortgage can probably be foreclosed in a state court, if not put within the jurisdiction of a federal court, by matters extrinsic from the patent law, it is safest to make such a mortgage conform to the mortgage laws of the state within which the mortgage is executed, and the laws of most, if not all the states require that a mortgage, shall be sealed, witnessed and acknowledged. The form of witnessing and acknowledgement given above, is the proper one for the state of Connecticut. In executing a mortgage in another state, the mortgage should conform, in these particulars, to the local law, which does not, however, vary much in the different states.

An acknowledgement before a Justice of the Peace, or a Notary Public, or other officer authorized to take acknowledgments, will be valid, but it is better to acknowledge before the Clerk of a court of record, for then his signature and seal will not generally need any further authentication for any purpose, while that of a justice, notary, or other officer, may. These mortgages require revenue stamps to the extent of fifty cents for every five hundred dollars of consideration, or fractional part thereof ; thus, a mortgage for $2,600 dollars would require $3.00 in stamps, five fifty cent stamps for the first $2,500, and fifty cents for $100 in excess thereof.

HINTS UPON INVENTION,

AND

KINDRED MATTERS.

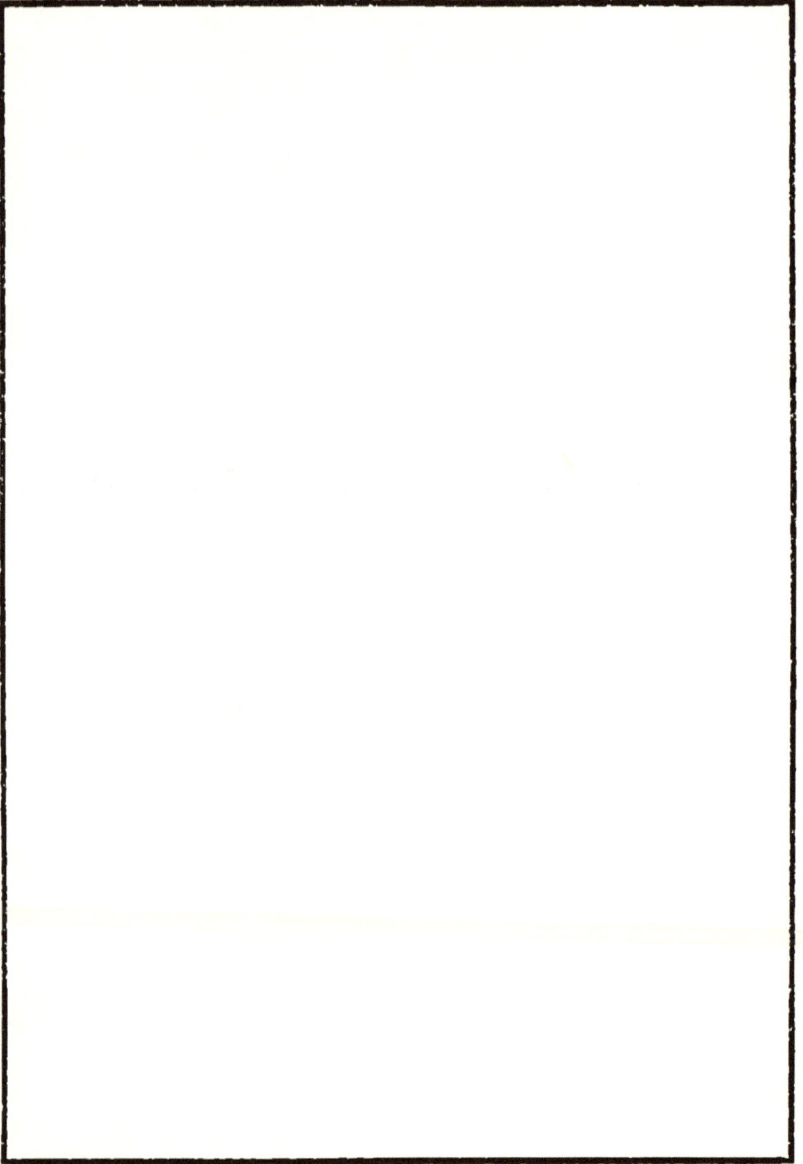

HOW TO INVENT.

It is beyond the scope of this work literally to teach how to invent; it is beyond the scope, or power, of any work to do this. No mere words can endow a brain with the subtle power of evolving from its inner self positive intellectual creations.

If this power could be imparted and conveyed by words, invention would soon cease to attract unusual attention, or to have any extraordinary money value; for, then, the science of invention would be taught in the schools, would be formulated in the books, and when an invention should be found needful, the person needing it would simply consult such books, or counsel with the professor of the science, and, *presto*, the required article would vault, full grown, upon the scene.

Invention, like poetry, sculpture and painting, is a gift, an endowment of nature, often rising to the height of genius. Like all other gifts, it can be cultivated and strengthened by exercise, till the acquired power as little resembles the original crude gift, as the oak, which has breasted a thousand storms, does the acorn from which it originally sprung.

This gift is, probably, the possession, in a greater or less degree, of all human beings of sound mind, nor does it seem to require inventive capacity of the highest order to produce important inventions. More than one invention, which has made its originator rich, famous, and all but immortal, has been the product of minds that lay no claim to kinship with genius. That quality of mind and character, which led Charles Goodyear to pursue for years, the *ignis fatuus* of hard rubber, till in a happy moment he stumbled upon the coveted secret, can hardly be called genius. Peter Cooper is well known as a successful inventor; he is not, however, it is believed, ranked as a genius. That inventors are sometimes geniuses, it is not necessary to say. The names of such as Whitney, Ericsson and Blanchard are too familiar. Still, it is true that most men and women can become inventors of that which will net them wealth, if not fame, by the aid of ATTENTION and PERSEVERANCE.

ATTENTION, constant, careful and thoughtful attention to what is going on in the world about one, will soon enable him to discover many little gaps which it is needful to fill with an invention, some small practical improvement, it may be, which, if it can be cheaply made, and effective in operation, will fill a general want, and thus command an extensive sale.

Having thus, by the aid of attention, discovered where an invention is needed, steady PERSEVERANCE in holding the matter in mind, all the while intently striving to devise a contrivance to fill the need, will, sooner or later, result in making the desired invention. The inventor, gifted by nature with a genius for his art, has, prominent among all his other powers, that of projecting before his mind's eye, upon an invisible background of imagination, a picture bold and sharp, of the offspring of his brain. But for all this, no one need be discouraged, if he spoils scores of fair sheets of paper with his sketches, and dozens of shapely blocks of wood with his knife and gimlet, before he demonstrates to his own satisfaction, that his invention will work.

PRINCIPAL REQUISITES OF AN INVENTION.

IT MUST WORK.—Upon this point of the practical working of a new device, an inventor can hardly be too severe or critical with himself—he must not give over his efforts till he is sure, beyond a doubt, that his invention will practically supply the want for which he has designed it, irrespective of any of those little allowances that inventors are apt to make for these children of their brain. There may be cases where an invention will be pecuniarily successful, when, though it may not work perfectly, it is yet the best thing so far found for the purpose for which it is designed. This is, obviously, a poor dependence, for it will probably be comparatively easy for some future inventor to perfect the incomplete invention, and thus destroy the first inventor's prospects.

IT MUST BE AS SIMPLE AS POSSIBLE.—There are many people, among them some inventors, who seem to think that a complicated arrangement of wheels and levers is the thing to be desired in a new invention. A greater mistake was never made; to attain the utmost simplicity is the test of genius in invention, and a prime desideratum. Simplicity in an article cheapens the cost of its production, and makes it a formidable competitor for its rivals. The difference of a cent or two in the first cost of an article often determines its success in the market.

Simplicity also tends to make an article grow in favor with those who use it ; it is the more easily understood, and less liable to breakage.

SMALL INVENTIONS.

He who aspires to be ranked as a great inventor may, perhaps, best apply himself to the production of some complicate mechanism, which shall take rank beside the steam engine, the solar engine, Blanchard's lathe for irregular forms, and the like, but those who will be satisfied with money returns may safely confine themselves to small inventions, which remedy some defect in some contrivance already in use, or supply some domestic, business or agricultural want.

Good toys, well pushed, are sure to prove remunerative ; the return ball is a favorite instance. Houschould articles have the most extensive market of anything; immense fortunes are, obviously, being made from the fruit jars now so common. Small articles require but little capital for their manufacture and introduction, while complicate and costly machines can only be successfully handled by parties of large means.

INVENTION AS A TRADE.

No one should make invention the main business of his life, his reliance for a livelihood, till he is possessed of so much of this world's goods, that he will not suffer, if he never realizes a dollar from his inventions. Otherwise he will be very likely to speedily have his face hard down upon the grindstone, which has for ages ground the faces of the poor, but, as yet, gives no sign of diminution in the speed of its revolution, or of wearing away by attrition. Let him devote every evening in the year, if he will, to invention, and ponder upon it at every spare moment in the day, but let him not relax his industry in his regular occupation, till he is in such circumstances that it matters but little whether he ever toils. The writer has in mind, in saying this, two men whom he has known, both of them gifted with considerable power of invention, men of many admirable qualities of character, good mechanics, whose services are always in demand, and who are capable of earning, with but ordinary industry, more than enough to support themselves and their families, in ease and comfort, but who are continually at their wits' end to pay their rent, and to procure but the commonest necessaries of life ; all because they will constantly neglect their regular work, to give form and substance to the creations of their brains. Not only does the course they pursue make them exceedingly uncomfortable in the mere matter of living, but it effectually deprives them of the chance of ever accumulating the small amount of funds necessary to perfect the smallest invention, and introduce it to the public notice.

CHEAP AND EFFICIENT PROTECTION.

In Mrs. Glass' Cook Book, under the head of " How to cook a Hare," the primary direction is, "First catch your hare." The inventor having caught his hare, in that he has made his invention, will next naturally proceed to cook it, that is, to realize some good from it. The first step in this direction is to secure protection, and a most advisable preliminary move is to assemble three or four intelligent and reliable friends, explain to them the model or drawing of the newly invented device, and then have them all sign a paper substantially like the following :

"Hartford, Conn., January 2d, 1871.

" John Smith has this day explained to us, so that we fully understand the same, the model (or drawing) of a Washing Machine that he claims to have invented.

JAMES JONES,
CHARLES BROWN,
HENRY ROBINSON."

This paper should be carefully kept, for in the future it may prove of great value in establishing the inventor's priority, in point of time, over some competitor. This proceeding will be found especially valuable, if any considerable time is allowed to elapse after the invention is made, before a patent is applied for.

74

The patent law allows an invention to go into public use and sale for two years before application for a patent, but it is probably never advisable to take advantage of this privilege, unless forced to it by necessity. It is better to keep the invention secret till the funds for procuring a patent can be acquired in some other way.

ABOUT SOLICITORS.

A few words about professional solicitors of patents may not be inappropriate, for it is advisable for almost all persons to avail themselves of the services of a faithful solicitor, in such securing patents.

In America, the practice of soliciting letters patent for inventions, has been, and is being largely carried on by unprofessional persons. Men who have neither paid earnest and persevering attention to the mechanic arts, nor have mastered the details of the legal profession, have deemed themselves fully competent to undertake this delicate and difficult work, which, beyond question, demands a thorough knowledge of all mechanical and chemical terms and processes in general use, a fair knowledge of the law in general, and an accurate knowledge of the patent law in particular.

This evil had become so aggravated, as to cause the Commissioner of Patents, Hon. S. S. Fisher, in his annual report for 1869, to take notice of it, as will be seen by the following

EXTRACT:

" Where establishments are organized for the purpose of procuring patents, they are apt to become more solicitous about the number than the quality of those which they obtain. This tendency is aggravated by those who solicit patents upon contingent fees, or who, without special training or qualifications, adopt this business as an incident to a claim agency, and press for patents as they press for back pay and pensions. Such men are often more desirous of obtaining a patent of any kind, and by any means, than they are of obtaining one which shall be of any value to their clients. Inventors are often poor, uneducated, and lacking in legal knowledge. They desire a cheap solicitor, and do not know how to choose a good one. They are pleased with the parchment and the seal, and are not themselves able to judge of the scope or value of the grant. Honest and skillful solicitors, with a thorough knowledge of the practice of the office, and of patent law, and who are able and willing to advise their clients as to the exact value of the patents which they can obtain for them, may be of much service to inventors. There are many such, but those who care for nothing but to give them something called a patent, that they may secure their own fee, have in too many instances proved a curse. To get rid of their client and of trouble, they have sometimes been content to take less than he was entitled to, while in many cases they have, with much self laudation, presented him with the shadow, when the substance was beyond his reach."

The following is from the Patent Office "Rules and Regulations" on this subject :

"Any person of intelligence and good moral character may appear as the attorney in fact, or agent of an applicant, upon filing a proper power of attorney. As the value of patents depends largely upon the careful preparation of the specification and claims, the assistance of competent counsel will, in most cases, be of advantage to the applicant, but the value of their services will be proportioned to their skill and honesty. So many persons have entered this profession of late years without experience, that too much care cannot be exercised in the selection of a competent man. The office cannot assume responsibility for the acts of attorneys, nor can it assist applicants in making a selection. It will, however, be a safe rule to distrust those who boast of the possession of special and peculiar facilities in the office, for procuring patents in a shorter time, or with more extended claims than others."

From which it is very easy to draw the following

MORAL.—In selecting a solicitor, find one who has had some special training for his business, and whose integrity is to be relied upon.

CENSUS

OF THE

UNITED STATES,

By States and Counties,

1870.

CENSUS

OF THE

United States, by Counties, for 1870.

ALABAMA—Area, 50,722 square miles.

County	Pop.	County	Pop.	County	Pop.
Autauga	11,623	Dallas	40,705	Marshall	9,871
Baker	6,194	De Kalb	7,126	Mobile	49,311
Baldwin	6,004	Elmore	14,477	Montgomery	43,704
Barbour	23,309	Escambia	4,041	Morgan	12,187
Bibb	7,469	Etowah	10,109	Monroe	14,214
Blount	9,945	Fayette	7,136	Perry	24,975
Bullock	24,474	Franklin	8,006	Pickens	17,690
Butler	14,981	Geneva	2,959	Pike	17,423
Calhoun	13,980	Greene	18,399	Randolph	12,006
Chambers	17,562	Hale	21,792	Russell	21,636
Cherokee	11,132	Henry	14,191	Sandford	8,893
Choctaw	12,676	Jackson	19,410	Shelby	12,218
Clark	14,663	Jefferson	12,345	St. Clair	9,360
Clay	9,560	Lauderdale	15,091	Sumter	24,109
Cleburne	8,017	Lawrence	16,658	Talladega	18,064
Coffee	6,171	Lee	21,750	Tallapoosa	16,963
Colbert	12,537	Limestone	15,017	Tuscaloosa	20,081
Conecub	9,374	Lowndes	25,719	Walker	6,543
Coosa	11,945	Macon	17,727	Washington	3,912
Covington	4,868	Madison	31,267	Wilcox	28,377
Crenshaw	11,156	Marengo	26,151	Winston	4,155
Dale	11,325	Marion	6,059	Total	996,992

ARKANSAS—Area, 52,198 square miles.

County	Pop.	County	Pop.	County	Pop.
Arkansas	8,268	Franklin	9,627	Montgomery	2,984
Ashley	8,042	Fulton	4,843	Newton	4,374
Benton	13,831	Grant	3,943	Oauchita	12,975
Boone	7,032	Green	7,573	Perry	2,685
Bradley	8,646	Hempstead	13,768	Phillips	15,372
Calhoun	3,853	Hot Springs	5,877	Pike	3,788
Carroll	5,780	Independence	14,566	Poinsett	1,720
Chicot	7,214	Izard	6,806	Polk	3,376
Clark	11,953	Jackson	7,268	Pope	8,386
Columbia	11,397	Jefferson	15,733	Prairie	5,604
Conway	8,112	Johnson	9,152	Pulaski	32,066
Crawford	8,957	Lafayette	9,139	Randolph	7,466
Crittenden	3,831	Lawrence	5,981	St. Francis	6,714
Craighead	4,577	Little River	3,236	Saline	3,911
Cross	3,915	Madison	8,231	Scott	7,483
Dallas	5,707	Marion	3,979	Searcy	5,614
Desha	6,125	Mississippi	3,633	Sebastian	12,940
Drew	9,960	Monroe	8,336	Sevier	4,492

Sharpe............	5,400	Washington........ 17,266	Woodruff 6,891
Unicn	10,571	White 10,347	Yell............... 8,048
Van Buren........	5,107	Total 484,471	

CALIFORNIA—Area, 188,981 square miles.

Alameda	24,237	Marin..............	6,903	Santa Barbara......	7,784
Alpine	685	Mariposa...........	4,572	Santa Clara	26,246
Amador............	9,582	Mendocino........	7,545	Santa Cruz........	8,743
Butte	11,403	Merced	2,807	Shasta	4,173
Calaveras	8,805	Mono	430	Siera	5,619
Colusa	6,165	Monterey	9,876	Siskiyou	6,848
Contra Costa......	8,461	Napa	7,163	Solano	16,871
Del Norte.........	2,022	Nevada	19,134	Sonoma............	19,819
El Dorado........	10,309	Placer	11,357	Stanislaus.........	6,499
Fresno	6,336	Plumas	4,489	Sutter	5,030
Humboldt	6,140	Sacramento	26,830	Tehama............	3,587
Inyo	1,956	San Bernardino....	3,988	Trinity	3,213
Kern	2,925	San Diego	4,951	Tulare	4,533
Klamath	1,686	San Francisco 149,473		Tuolumne	8,150
Lake	2,969	San Joaquin	21,050	Yolo	9,899
Lassen	1,327	San L. Obispo......	4,772	Yuba	10,851
Los Angelos.......	15,309	San Mateo	6,635	Total 560,247	

CONNECTICUT—Area, 4,674 square miles.

Fairfield 95,276	Middlesex..........36,099	Tolland 22,000	
Hartford.........109,007	New Haven.......121,257	Windham 38,518	
Litchfield 48,727	New London........66,570	Total 337,454	

DELAWARE—Area, 2,120 square miles.

Kent...............29,804	New Castle.........63,515	Sussex..............31,696
Total..125,015		

FLORIDA—Area, 59,268 square miles.

Alachua 17,328	Hernando..........	2,938	Nassau	4,247	
Baker..............	1,325	Hillsboro	3,216	Orange.............	2,195
Bradford	3,671	Holmes	1,572	Polk	3,169
Brevard	1,216	Jackson	9,528	Putnam............	3,821
Calhoun	998	Jefferson...........13,398		Santa Rosa........	3,312
Clay	2,098	La Fayette.........	1,783	St. John's..........	2,618
Columbia	7,335	Leon...............15,236		Sumter	2,952
Dade..............	85	Levy	2,018	Suwannee	3,556
Duval 11,921	Liberty	1,050	Taylor	1,453
Escambia	7,817	Madison............11,121		Volusia	1,723
Franklin..........	1,256	Manatee	1,931	Wakulla	2,506
Gadsden	9,802	Marion 10,804		Walton	3,041
Hamilton	5,749	Monroe	5,657	Washington........	2,302
Total...187,748					

GEORGIA—Area, 58,000 square miles.

Appling............	5,086	Bibb...............21,255		Calhoun............	5,503
Baker	6,843	Brooks	8,342	Camden	4,615
Baldwin 10,618	Bryan	5,252	Campbell	9,176
Banks.............	4,973	Bullock	5,610	Carroll............11,782
Bartow 16,566	Burke 17,679		Catoosa	4,409
Berrien	4,518	Butts	6,941	Charlton	1,897

Chatham 41,279	Hall 9,607	Pike 10,905
Chattahoochee 6,059	Hancock 11,317	Polk 7,822
Chattooga 6,902	Haralson 4,004	Pulaski 11,940
Cherokee 10,399	Harris 13,284	Putnam 10,461
Clarke 12,941	Hart 6,783	Quitman 4,150
Clay 5,493	Heard 7,866	Rabun 3,256
Clayton 5,477	Henry 10,102	Randolph 10,561
Clinch 3,945	Houston 20,406	Richmond 25,724
Cobb 13,814	Irwin 1,837	Schley 5,129
Coffee 3,192	Jackson 11,181	Scriven 9,175
Colquitt 1,654	Jasper 10,439	Spalding 10,205
Columbia 13,529	Jefferson 12,150	Stewart 14,204
Coweta 15,875	Johnson 2,964	Sumter 16,559
Crawford 7,557	Jones 9,436	Tallot 11,913
Dade 3,033	Laurens 7,834	Taliaferro 4,596
Dawson 4,369	Lee 9,567	Tatnall 4,860
Decatur 15,183	Liberty 7,688	Taylor 7,143
De Kalb 10,014	Lincoln 5,413	Telfair 3,245
Dooly 9,790	Lowndes 8,321	Terrell 9,053
Dougherty 11,517	Lumpkin 5,161	Thomas 14,523
Early 6,998	Macon 11,458	Towns 2,780
Echols 1,978	Madison 5,227	Troup 17,632
Effingham 4,214	Marion 8,003	Twiggs 8,545
Elbert 9,249	McIntosh.......... 4,491	Union 5,267
Emanuel 6,134	Meriwether 13,756	Upson 9,430
Fannin 5,429	Miller 3,091	Walker 9,925
Fayette 8,221	Milton 4,284	Walton 11,038
Floyd 17,230	Mitchell 6,633	Ware 2,286
Forsyth 7,983	Monroe 17,213	Warren 10,545
Franklin 7,893	Montgomery 3,586	Washington 15,842
Fulton 33,446	Morgan 10,696	Wayne 2,177
Gilmer 6,644	Murray 6,500	Webster 4,677
Glascock 2,736	Muscogee 16,663	White 4,606
Glynn 5,376	Newton 14,615	Whitfield 10,117
Gordon 9,268	Oglethorpe........ 11,782	Wilcox 2,439
Greene............ 12,454	Paulding.......... 7,639	Wilkes 11,796
Gwinnett ....: 12,431	Pickens 5,317	Wilkinson 9,383
Habersham 6,322	Pierce 2,778	Worth 3,778
Total...1,184,109

ILLINOIS—Area, 55,405 square miles.

Adams............. 56,362	Cowles............ 25,235	Fulton............ 38,291
Alexander 10,564	Cook 349,966	Gallatin........... 11,134
Bond 13,152	Crawford 13,889	Greene 20,277
Boone 12,942	Cumberland 12,223	Grundy 14,938
Brown............. 12,205	De Kalb........... 23,265	Hamilton 13,014
Bureau 32,415	De Witt 14,768	Hancock 35,935
Calhoun 6,562	Douglas........... 13,484	Hardin 5,113
Carroll............ 16,705	Du Page 16,685	Henderson........ 12,582
Cass 11,580	Edgar 21,450	Henry 35,506
Champaign 32,737	Edwards 7,565	Iroquois 25,782
Christian 20,363	Effingham 15,653	Jackson........... 19,634
Clark 18,719	Fayette 19,638	Jasper 11,234
Clay 15,875	Ford.............. 9,103	Jefferson 17,864
Clinton 16,285	Franklin.......... 12,652	Jersey............ 15,054

Jo Daviess........ 27,820	McHenry 23,762	Sangamon 46,352
Johnson 11,248	McLean 53,988	Schuyler 17,419
Kane 39,091	Menard 11,735	Scott 10,530
Kankakee 24,352	Mercer 18,769	Shelby 25,476
Kendall 12,399	Monroe 12,982	Stark 10,751
Knox 39,522	Montgomery 25,314	St. Clair 51,068
Lake 21,014	Morgan 28,463	Stephenson 30,608
La Salle 60,792	Moultrie 10,385	Tazewell 27,903
Lawrence 12,533	Ogle 27,492	Union 16,518
Lee 27,171	Peoria 47,540	Vermillion 30,388
Livingston 31,471	Perry 13,723	Wabash 8,841
Logan 23,053	Piatt 10,953	Warren 23,174
Macon 26,481	Pike 30,768	Washington 17,599
Macoupin 32,726	Pope 11,437	Wayne 19,758
Madison 44,131	Pulaski 8,752	White 16,846
Marion 20,622	Putnam 6,280	Whitesides 27,503
Marshall 16,956	Randolph 20,859	Will 43,013
Mason 16,184	Richland 12,803	Williamson 17,329
Massac 9,581	Rock Island 29,783	Winnebago 29,301
McDonough 26,509	Saline 12,714	Woodford 18,956

Total..2,539,891

INDIANA—Area, 33,809 Square miles.

Adams............. 11,382	Hendricks 20,277	Pike 13,779
Allen............. 43,494	Henry 22,986	Porter 13,942
Bartholomew 21,133	Howard 15,847	Posey 19,185
Benton 5,615	Huntington 19,036	Pulaski 7,801
Blackford......... 6,272	Jackson........... 18,974	Putnam............ 21,514
Boone 22,593	Jasper 6,354	Randolph 22,862
Brown............. 8,681	Jay 15,000	Ripley 20,977
Carroll........... 16,152	Jefferson 29,741	Rush 17,626
Cass 24,193	Jennings 16,218	Scott 7,873
Clarke 24,770	Johnson 18,366	Shelby............ 21,892
Clay.............. 19,084	Knox 21,562	Spencer........... 17,998
Clinton 17,330	Kosciusko 23,531	Starke 3,888
Crawford 9,851	La Grange 14,148	Steuben 12,854
Daviess........... 16,747	Lake ....: 12,339	St. Joseph 25,322
Dearborn 24,116	La Porte 27,062	Sullivan 18,453
Decatur........... 19,053	Lawrence 14,628	Switzerland....... 12,134
De Kalb........... 17,167	Madison 22,770	Tippecanoe 33,515
Delaware 19,030	Marion 71,939	Tipton............ 11,953
Dubois 12,597	Marshall 20,211	Union 6,341
Elkhart 26,026	Martin 11,103	Vanderburg 33,145
Fayette 10,476	Miami 21,052	Vermillion......... 10,840
Floyd............. 23,300	Monroe............ 14,168	Vigo 33,594
Fountain 16,389	Montgomery 23,765	Wabash 21,305
Franklin.......... 20,223	Morgan............ 17,528	Warren 10,204
Fulton............ 12,726	Newton 5,829	Warrick 17,653
Gibson 17,371	Noble 20,389	Washington 18,495
Grant............. 18,487	Ohio 5,837	Wayne 34,048
Greene 19,514	Orange 13,497	Wells 13,585
Hamilton 20,882	Owen 16,137	White 10,554
Hancock 15,123	Parke............. 18,166	Whitley 14,399
Harrison.......... 19,913	Perry............. 14,801	Total...... 1,680,637

IOWA—Area, 50,914 square miles.

County	Pop.	County	Pop.	County	Pop.
Adair	3,982	Floyd	10,768	Monona	3,654
Adams	4,614	Franklin	4,738	Monroe	12,724
Allamakee	17,868	Fremont	11,174	Montgomery	5,934
Appanoose	16,456	Greene	4,627	Muscatine	21,688
Audubon	1,212	Grundy	6,399	O'Brien	715
Benton	22,454	Guthrie	7,061	Page	9,975
Black Hawk	21,706	Hamilton	6,055	Palo Alto	1,336
Boone	14,584	Hancock	999	Plymouth	2,199
Bremer	12,528	Hardin	13,684	Pocahontas	1,446
Buchanan	17,034	Harrison	8,931	Polk	27,857
Buena Vista	1,585	Henry	21,463	Pottawattamie	16,893
Butler	9,951	Howard	6,282	Poweshiek	15,581
Calhoun	1,602	Humboldt	2,596	Ringgold	5,691
Carroll	2,451	Ida	226	Sac	1,411
Cass	5,464	Iowa	16,644	Scott	38,599
Cedar	19,731	Jackson	22,619	Shelby	2,540
Cerro Gordo	4,722	Jasper	22,116	Sioux	576
Cherokee	1,967	Jefferson	17,839	Story	11,651
Chickasaw	10,180	Johnson	24,898	Tama	16,131
Clarke	8,735	Jones	19,731	Taylor	6,989
Clay	1,523	Keokuk	19,434	Union	5,986
Clayton	27,771	Kossuth	3,351	Van Buren	17,672
Clinton	35,357	Lee	37,210	Wapello	22,346
Crawford	2,530	Linn	28,852	Warren	17,980
Dallas	12,019	Louisa	12,877	Washington	18,952
Davis	15,565	Lucas	10,388	Wayne	11,287
Decatur	12,018	Lyon	221	Webster	10,484
Delaware	17,432	Madison	13,884	Winnebago	1,562
Des Moines	27,256	Mahaska	22,508	Winneshiek	23,570
Dickinson	1,389	Marion	24,436	Woodbury	6,172
Dubuque	38,969	Marshall	17,576	Worth	2,892
Emmett	1,392	Mills	8,718	Wright	2,392
Fayette	16,973	Mitchell	9,582	Total	1,191,792

KANSAS—Area, 78,418 square miles.

County	Pop.	County	Pop.	County	Pop.
Allen	7,022	Doniphan	13,969	Lyon	8,014
Anderson	5,220	Douglass	20,592	Marion	768
Atchison	15,507	Ellis	1,336	Marshall	6,901
Barton	2	Ellsworth	1,185	McPherson	738
Bourbon	15,076	Ford	427	Miami	11,725
Brown	6,823	Franklin	10,385	Mitchell	485
Butler	3,035	Greenwood	3,484	Montgomery	7,564
Chase	1,975	Howard	2,704	Morris	2,225
Cherokee	11,038	Jackson	6,053	Nemeha	7,339
Clay	2,942	Jefferson	12,526	Neosho	10,206
Cloud	2,323	Jewell	207	Ness	2
Coffey	6,201	Johnson	13,084	Osage	7,648
Cowley	1,175	Labette	9,973	Osborne	33
Crawford	8,160	Leavenworth	32,444	Ottawa	2,127
Davis	5,526	Lincoln	516	Pawnee	179
Dickinson	3,043	Linn	13,174	Pottawattamie	7,848

Republic	1,281	Shawnee	13,131	Wallace	538
Rice	5	Smith	66	Washington	4,081
Riley	5,105	Sumner	22	Wilson	6,694
Russell	156	Trego	166	Woodson	3,827
Saline	4,246	Wabaunsee	3,362	Wyandotte	10,015
Sedgwick	1,095			Total	364,399

KENTUCKY—Area, 37,680 square miles.

Adair	11,065	Graves	19,398	Menifee	1,986
Allen	10,296	Grayson	11,580	Mercer	13,144
Anderson	5,449	Green	9,379	Metcalfe	7,934
Ballard	12,576	Greenup	11,463	Monroe	9,231
Barren	17,780	Hancock	6,591	Montgomery	7,557
Bath	10,145	Hardin	15,705	Morgan	5,975
Boone	10,696	Harlan	4,415	Muhlenburg	12,638
Bourbon	14,863	Harrison	12,993	Nelson	14,804
Boyd	8,573	Hart	13,687	Nicholas	9,129
Boyle	9,515	Henderson	18,457	Ohio	15,561
Bracken	11,409	Henry	11,066	Oldham	9,027
Breathit	5,672	Hickman	8,453	Owen	14,309
Breckenridge	13,440	Hopkins	13,827	Owsley	3,889
Bullitt	7,781	Jackson	4,547	Pendleton	14,030
Butler	9,404	Jefferson	118,953	Perry	4,274
Caldwell	10,826	Jessamine	8,638	Pike	9,562
Callaway	9,410	John Bell	3,731	Powell	2,599
Campbell	27,406	Johnson	7,494	Pulaski	17,670
Carroll	6,189	Kenton	36,096	Robertson	5,399
Carter	7,509	Knox	8,294	Rock Castle	7,145
Casey	8,884	La Rue	8,235	Rowan	2,991
Christian	23,227	Laurel	6,016	Russell	5,809
Clark	10,882	Lawrence	8,497	Scott	11,607
Clay	8,297	Lee	3,058	Shelby	15,733
Clinton	6,497	Letcher	4,608	Simpson	9,573
Crittenden	9,381	Lewis	9,115	Spencer	5,956
Cumberland	7,690	Lincoln	10,947	Taylor	8,226
Daviess	20,714	Livingston	8,200	Todd	12,612
Edmonson	4,459	Logan	20,429	Trigg	13,686
Elliott	4,433	Lyon	6,233	Trimble	5,577
Estill	9,198	Madison	19,543	Union	13,640
Fayette	26,656	Magoffin	4,684	Warren	21,742
Fleming	13,398	Marion	12,838	Washington	12,464
Floyd	7,877	Marshall	9,455	Wayne	10,602
Franklin	15,300	Mason	18,126	Webster	10,937
Fulton	6,161	McCracken	13,988	Whitley	8,279
Gallatin	5,074	McLean	7,614	Wolfe	3,603
Garrard	10,376	Meade	9,485	Woodford	8,240
Grant	9,529			Total	1,321,011

LOUISIANA—Area, 41,255 square miles.

Ascension	11,577	Bossier	12,675	Cameron	1,591
Assumption	13,224	Caddo	21,714	Carroll	10,110
Avoyelles	12,926	Calcasieu	6,733	Catahoula	8,475
Bienville	10,636	Caldwell	4,820	Claiborne	20,240

Concordia 9,977	Morehouse......... 9,387	St. Landry........ 25,553
De Soto........... 14,962	Natchitoches 18,265	St. Martin 9,370
East Baton Rouge.. 17,816	Orleans 191,418	St. Mary........... 13,860
East Feliciana...... 13,499	Ouachita 11,582	St. Tammany 5,586
Franklin.......... 5,078	Plaquemines 10,552	Tangipahoa 7,928
Graut............. 4,517	Point Coupee 12,981	Tensas............. 12,419
Iberia 9,042	Rapides............ 18,015	Terrebonne 12,441
Iberville 12,347	Richland.......... 5,110	Union 11,685
Jackson........... 7,646	Sabine 6,456	Vermillion........ 4,528
Jefferson 17,767	St. Bernard........ 3,553	Washington....... 3,330
Lafayette 10,388	St. Charles........ 4,857	West Baton Rouge.. 5,114
Lafourche 14,719	St. Helena 5,423	West Feliciona..... 10,499
Livingston........ 4,026	St. James 10,152	Winn 5,954
Madison 8,600	St. John the Baptist 6,762	Total........726,915

MAINE—Area, 31,766 square miles.

Androscoggin...... 35,866	Knox 30,823	Sagadahoc 18,803
Aroostook 29,609	Lincoln............ 25,597	Somerset 34,611
Cumberland 82,021	Oxford 33,488	Waldo 34,522
Franklin.......... 18,811	Penobscot 75,150	Washington........ 43,343
Hancock 36,495	Piscataquis 14,403	York 69,174
Kennebec.......... 53,203	Total.................626,915	

MARYLAND—Area, 11,124 square miles.

Allegany 38,536	Dorchester......... 19,458	Queen 16,171
Anne Arundel...... 24,457	Frederick.......... 47,572	Saint Mary's...... 14,944
Baltimore..........330,741	Harford 22,605	Somerset 18,190
Calvert 9,865	Howard............ 14,150	Talbot 16,137
Caroline 12,101	Kent 17,102	Washington........ 34,712
Carroll............ 28,619	Montgomery....... 20,563	Wicomico......... 15,802
Cecil.............. 25,874	Prince George's.... 21,138	Worcester 16,419
Charles 15,738	Total.....................780,894	

MASSACHUSETTS—Area, 7,800 square miles.

Barnstable........ 32,774	Franklin............32,6''	Norfolk............ 89,443
Berkshire.......... 64,827	Hampden.......... 78,409	Plymouth.......... 65,365
Bristol............102,886	Hampshire........ 44,388	Suffolk............270,802
Dukes 3,787	Middlesex 274,353	Worcester 192,716
Essex..............200,843	Nantucket 4,123	Total.....1,457,351

MICHIGAN—Area, 56,243 square miles.

Alcona............ 696	Chippewa.......... 1,689	Ionia 27,681
Allegan 32,105	Clare 366	Iosco 3,163
Alpena............ 2,756	Clinton 22,845	Isabella 4,113
Antrim 1,985	Delta 2,542	Jackson............ 36,047
Barry 22,199	Eaton.............. 25,171	Kalamazoo........ 32,054
Bay............... 15,900	Emmet 1,211	Kalkaska.......... 424
Benzie............ 2,184	Genesee 33,900	Kent 50,403
Berrien 35,104	Grand Traverse.... 4,443	Keweenaw 4,205
Branch............ 26,226	Gratiot 11,810	Lake.............. 548
Calhoun 36,569	Hillsdale........... 31,684	Lapeer............ 21,345
Cass 21,094	Houghton.......... 13,879	Leelanaw 4,576
Charlevoix 1,724	Huron............. 9,049	Lenawee 45,595
Cheboygan........ 2,196	Ingham............ 25,268	Livingston......... 19,336

Mackinac 1,716	Montcalm 13,629	Saginaw 39,097
Macomb 27,616	Muskegon 14,894	Sanilac 14,562
Manistee.......... 6,074	Newaygo.......... 7,294	Shiawassee........ 20,858
Manitou 891	Oakland........... 40,867	St. Clair 36,661
Marquette......... 15,033	Oceana 7,222	St. Joseph 26,275
Mason 3,263	Ogemaw 12	Tuscola........... 13,714
Mecosta.......... 5,642	Ontonagon........ 2,845	Van Buren........ 28,829
Menominee 1,791	Osceola 2,093	Washtenaw........ 41,434
Midland 3,285	Oscoda............ 70	Wayne.............119,038
Missaukee 130	Ottawa............ 26,651	Wexford 650
Monroe........... 27,483	Presque Isle].......355	Total.....1,184,059

MINNESOTA—Area, 95,274 square miles.

Aitkin 178	Hennepin.......... 21,566	Pope 2,691
Anoka 3,940	Houston 14,936	Ramsey........... 23,085
Becker 308	Isanti.............. 2,035	Redwood 1,829
Beltrami.......... 80	Itasca............. 96	Renville 3,219
Benton 1,558	Jackson 1,825	Rice 16,083
Big Stone......... 24	Kanabec.......... 93	Rock 138
Blue Earth 17,302	Kandiyohi 1,760	Scott 11,042
Brown............ 6,396	Lac qui Parle 145	Sherburne 2,050
Carlton 286	Lake 135	Sibley 6,725
Carver............ 11,586	Le Sueur 11,607	Stearns 14,206
Cass 380	Martin............ 3,867	Steele............. 8,271
Chippewa 1,467	McLeod 5,643	Stevens 174
Chisago........... 4,358	Meeker 6,090	St. Louis 4,561
Clay 92	Mille Lac 1,109	Todd 2,036
Cottonwood....... 534	Monongalia 3,160	Traverse.......... 13
Crow Wing 200	Morrison 1,681	Wabashaw 15,859
Dakota 16,312	Mower............. 10,447	Wadena............ 6
Dodge 8,598	Murray............ 209	Waseca............ 7,854
Douglass.......... 4,239	Nicollet 8,362	Washington........ 11,809
Faribault 9,940	Nobles............ 117	Watonwan 2,426
Fillmore 24,887	Olmsted 19,793	Wilkin............. 295
Freeborn 10,578	Otter Tail......... 1,968	Winona............ 22,319
Goodhue.......... 22,618	Pembina........... 64	Wright 9,457
Grant............. 340	Pine 648,	Total 439,706

MISSISSIPPI—Area, 47,156 square miles.

Adams............ 19,084	Coahoma 7,144	Itawamba......... 7,812
Alcorn 10,431	Copiah 20,608	Jackson........... 4,362
Amite 10,973	Covington 4,753	Jasper 10,884
Attala 14,776	De Soto........... 32,021	Jefferson 13,848
Bolivar 9,732	Franklin........... 7,498	Jones............. 3,313
Calhoun 10,561	Greene............ 2,038	Kemper 12,920
Carroll 21,047	Grenada 10,571	Lafayette 18,802
Chickasaw 19,899	Hancock 4,239	Lauderdale 13,462
Choctaw 16,988	Harrison.......... 5,795	Lawrence 6,620
Claiborne 13,586	Hinds 30,488	Leake 8,496
Clark 7,505	Holmes 19,370	Lee............... 15,955
	Issaquena.......... 6,887	Lincoln........... 10,184

Lowndes... 30,502	Perry... 2,694	Tippah... 20,727
Madison... 20,948	Pike... 11,303	Tishemingo... 7,350
Marion... 4,211	Pontotoc... 12,525	Tunica... 5,358
Marshall... 29,416	Prentiss... 9,348	Warren... 26,769
Monroe... 22,631	Rankin... 12,977	Washington... 14,569
Neshoba... 7,439	Scott... 7,847	Wayne... 4,206
Newton... 10,067	Simpson... 5,718	Wilkinson... 12,705
Noxubee... 20,905	Smith... 7,126	Winston... 8,984
Oktibbeha... 14,891	Sunflower... 5,015	Yalabusha... 13,254
Panola... 20,754	Tallahatchie... 7,852	Yazoo... 17,279
	Total...	827,922

MISSOURI—Area, 67,380 square miles.

Adair... 11,448	Greene... 21,549	Ozark... 3,363
Andrew... 15,137	Grundy... 10,567	Pemiscot... 2,059
Atchison... 8,440	Harrison... 14,635	Perry... 9,877
Audrain... 12,307	Henry... 17,401	Pettis... 18,706
Barry... 10,373	Hickory... 6,452	Phelps... 10,506
Barton... 5,087	Holt... 11,652	Pike... 23,076
Bates... 15,960	Howard... 17,233	Platte... 17,352
Benton... 11,322	Howell... 4,218	Polk... 12,445
Bollinger... 8,162	Iron... 6,278	Pulaski... 4,714
Boone... 20,765	Jackson... 55,041	Putnam... 11,217
Buchanan... 35,109	Jasper... 14,928	Ralls... 10,510
Butler... 4,298	Jefferson... 15,380	Randolph... 15,908
Caldwell... 11,390	Johnson... 24,648	Ray... 18,700
Callaway... 19,202	Knox... 10,974	Reynolds... 3,756
Camdem... 6,108	Laclede... 9,380	Ripley... 3,175
Cape Girardeau... 17,558	Lafayette... 22,623	Saline... 21,672
Carroll... 17,446	Lawrence... 13,067	Schuyler... 8,820
Carter... 1,455	Lewis... 15,114	Scotland... 10,670
Cass... 19,296	Lincoln... 15,960	Scott... 7,317
Cedar... 9,474	Linn... 15,900	Shannon... 2,339
Chariton... 19,136	Livingston... 16,730	Shelby... 10,119
Christian... 6,707	Macon... 23,230	St. Charles... 21,304
Clarke... 13,667	Madison... 5,849	St. Clare... 6,742
Clay... 15,564	Maries... 5,916	Ste. Genevieve... 8,384
Clinton... 14,063	Marion... 23,780	St. Francois... 9,742
Cole... 10,292	McDonald... 5,226	St. Louis... 351,189
Cooper... 20,692	Mercer... 11,557	Stoddard... 8,535
Crawford... 7,982	Miller... 6,616	Stone... 3,253
Dade... 8,683	Mississippi... 4,982	Sullivan... 11,907
Dallas... 8,383	Moniteau... 11,375	Taney... 4,407
Daviess... 14,410	Monroe... 17,149	Texas... 9,618
De Kalb... 9,858	Montgomery... 10,405	Vernon... 11,247
Dent... 6,357	Morgan... 8,434	Warren... 9,673
Douglass... 3,915	New Madrid... 6,357	Washington... 11,719
Dunklin... 5,982	Newton... 12,821	Wayne... 6,068
Franklin... 30,098	Nodaway... 14,751	Webster... 10,434
Gasconade... 10,093	Oregon... 3,287	Worth... 5,004
Gentry... 11,607	Osage... 10,793	Wright... 5,684
	Total...	1,721,295

NEBRASKA—Area, 75,995 square miles.

Adams... 19	Blackbird... 31	Buffalo... 193

Burt	2,847	Jackson	9
Butler	1,290	Jefferson	2,440
Cass	8,151	Johnson	3,429
Cedar	1,032	Kearney	58
Cheyenne	190	Lancaster	7,074
Clay	54	L'Eau qui Court	261
Colfax	1,424	Lincoln	17
Cuming	2,964	Lyon	78
Dakota	2,040	Madison	1,133
Dawson	103	Merrick	557
Dixon	1,345	Monroe	235
Dodge	4,212	Nemaha	7,593
Douglass	19,982	Nuckolls	8
Fillmore	238	Otoe	12,345
Franklin	26	Pawnee	4,171
Gage	3,350	Pierce	152
Grant	484	Platte	1,899
Hall	1,057	Polk	136
Hamilton	130	Richardson	9,780
Harrison	631	Saline	3,106

Sarpy	2,913
Saunders	4,547
Seward	2,953
Stanton	636
Taylor	97
Washington	4,452
Wayne	182
Webster	16
York	604
Unorganized North-	
west Tcerritory..	52
Unorganized Terri-	
tory west of Mad-	
ison County	183
Winnebago Indian	
Reservation	31
Pawnee Indian res-	
ervation	44
Total	122,993

NEVADA—Area, 112,090 square miles.

Churchill	196	Lander	2,815
Douglas	1,215	Lincoln	2,985
Elko	3,447	Lyon	1,837
Esmeralda	1,553	Nye	1,087
Humboldt	1,916	Ormsby	3,668

Roop	133
Storey	11,359
Washoe	3,091
White Pine	7,189
Total	42,491

NEW HAMPSHIRE—Area, 9,280 square miles.

Belknap	17,681	Grafton	39,103
Carroll	17,332	Hillsborough	64,238
Cheshire	27,265	Merrimack	42,151
Coos	14,932		

Rockingham	47,297
Strafford	30,243
Sullivan	18,058
Total	318,300

NEW JERSEY—Area, 3,320 square miles.

Atlantic	14,093	Gloucester	21,562
Bergen	30,122	Hudson	129,067
Burlington	53,639	Hunterdon	36,963
Camden	46,193	Mercer	46,386
Cape May	8,349	Middlesex	45,029
Cumberland	34,665	Monmouth	46,195
Essex	143,839	Morris	43,137

Ocean	13,628
Passaic	46,416
Salem	23,940
Somerset	23,510
Sussex	23,168
Union	41,859
Warren	34,336
Total	906,096

NEW YORK—Area, 47,000 square miles.

Albany	133,052	Clinton	47,947
Allegany	40,814	Columbia	47,044
Broome	44,103	Cortland	25,173
Cattaraugus	43,909	Delaware	42,972
Cayuga	59,550	Dutchess	74,041
Chautauqua	59,327	Erie	178,699
Chemung	35,281	Essex	29,042
Chenango	40,564	Franklin	30,271

Fulton	27,064
Genesee	31,606
Greene	31,832
Hamilton	2,960
Herkimer	39,929
Jefferson	65,415
Kings	419,921
Lewis	28,699

Livingston	38,309	Otsego	48,967	St. Lawrence	84,826
Madison	43,522	Putnam	15,420	Suffolk	46,924
Monroe	117,868	Queens	73,803	Sullivan	34,550
Montgomery	34,457	Rensselaer	99,549	Tioga	30,572
New York	942,292	Richmond	33,029	Tompkins	33,178
Niagara	50,437	Rockland	25,213	Ulster	84,075
Oneida	110,008	Saratoga	51,529	Warren	22,592
Onondaga	104,183	Schenectady	21,347	Washington	49,568
Ontario	45,108	Schoharie	33,340	Wayne	47,710
Orange	80,902	Schuyler	18,989	Westchester	131,348
Orleans	27,689	Seneca	27,823	Wyoming	29,164
Oswego	77,941	Steuben	67,717	Yates	19,595
Total					4,382,759

NORTH CAROLINA—Area, 50,704 square miles.

Alamance	11,874	Edgecombe	22,970	Northampton	14,749
Alexander	6,868	Forsyth	13,050	Onslow	7,569
Alleghany	3,691	Franklin	14,134	Orange	17,507
Anson	12,428	Gaston	12,602	Pasquotank	8,131
Ashe	9,573	Gates	7,724	Perquimans	7,945
Beaufort	13,011	Granville	24,831	Person	11,170
Bertie	12,950	Greene	8,687	Pitt	17,276
Bladen	12,831	Guilford	21,736	Polk	4,319
Brunswick	7,754	Halifax	20,408	Randolph	17,551
Buncombe	15,412	Harnett	8,895	Richmond	12,882
Burke	9,777	Haywood	7,921	Robeson	16,262
Cabarrus	11,954	Henderson	7,706	Rockingham	15,708
Caldwell	8,476	Hertford	9,273	Rowan	16,810
Camden	5,361	Hyde	6,445	Rutherford	13,121
Carteret	9,010	Iredell	16,931	Sampson	16,436
Caswell	16,081	Jackson	6,683	Stanley	8,315
Catawba	10,984	Johnston	16,897	Stokes	11,208
Chatham	19,723	Jones	5,002	Surry	11,252
Cherokee	8,080	Lenoir	10,434	Transylvania	3,536
Chowan	6,450	Lincoln	9,573	Tyrrell	4,173
Clay	2,461	Macon	6,615	Union	12,217
Cleaveland	12,696	Madison	8,192	Wake	35,617
Columbus	8,474	Martin	9,647	Warren	17,768
Craven	20,516	McDowell	7,592	Washington	6,516
Cumberland	17,035	Mecklenburg	24,299	Watauga	5,287
Currituck	5,131	Mitchell	4,705	Wayne	18,144
Dare	2,778	Montgomery	7,487	Wilkes	15,539
Davidson	17,414	Moore	12,040	Wilson	12,258
Davie	9,620	Nash	11,077	Yadkin	10,697
Duplin	15,542	New Hanover	27,978	Yancy	5,909
Total					1,071,361

OHIO—Area, 39,964 square miles

Adams	20,750	Brown	30,802	Columbiana	38,299
Allen	23,623	Butler	39,912	Coshocton	23,600
Ashland	21,933	Carroll	14,491	Crawford	25,556
Ashtabula	32,517	Champaign	24,188	Cuyahoga	132,010
Athens	23,768	Clark	32,070	Darke	32,278
Auglaize	20,041	Clermont	34,268	Defiance	15,719
Belmont	39,714	Clinton	21,914	Delaware	25,175

Erie 28,188	Licking 35,756	Portage 24,584
Fairfield 31,138	Logan 23,028	Preble 21,809
Fayette 17,170	Lorain 30,308	Putnam 17,081
Franklin 63,019	Lucas 46,722	Richland 32,516
Fulton 17,789	Madison 15,633	Ross 37,097
Gallia 25,545	Mahoning 31,001	Sandusky 25,503
Geauga 14,190	Marion 16,184	Scioto 29,302
Greene 28,038	Medina 20,092	Seneca 30,827
Guernsey 23,838	Meigs 31,465	Shelby 20,748
Hamilton 260,370	Mercer 17,254	Stark 52,508
Hancock 23,847	Miami 32,740	Summit 34,674
Hardin 18,714	Monroe 25,779	Trumbull.......... 38,659
Harrison........... 18,682	Montgomery 64,006	Tuscarawas 53,840
Henry 14,028	Morgan............ 20,363	Union 18,730
Highland 29,133	Morrow............ 18,583	Van Wert......... 15,823
Hocking 17,925	Muskingum 44,886	Vinton............. 15,027
Holmes 18,177	Noble............. 19,949	Warren 26,689
Huron 28,532	Ottawa............ 13,364	Washington........ 40,609
Jackson........... 21,759	Paulding.......... 8,544	Wayne............. 35,116
Jefferson 29,188	Perry............. 18,453	Williams.......... 20,991
Knox 26,333	Pickaway 24,875	Wood............. 24,596
Lake 15,935	Pike 15,447	Wyandot.......... 18,553
Lawrence 31,380		Total........................2,665,260

OREGON—Area, 102,606 square miles.

Baker 2,804	Grant............. 2,251	Polk 4,701
Benton 4,584	Jackson 4,778	Tillamook 408
Clackamas 5,993	Josephine 1,204	Umatilla 2,916
Clatsop 1,255	Lane 6,426	Union 2,552
Columbia 863	Linn 8,717	Wasco 2,509
Coos.............. 1,644	Marion 9,965	Washington........ 4,261
Curry 504	Multnomah 11,510	Yam Hill 5,012
Douglas 6,066		Total........................90,923

PENNSYLVANIA—Area, 46,000 square miles.

Adams............. 30,315	Cumberland 43,912	McKean 8,825
Alleghany 262,204	Dauphin........... 60,740	Mercer 49,977
Armstrong........ 43,382	Delaware 39,403	Mifflin 17,508
Beaver 36,148	Elk 8,488	Monroe.......... 18,362
Bedford 29,635	Erie 65,973	Montgomery 81,612
Berks.............106,701	Fayette 43,284	Montour ... 15,344
Blair 38,051	Forest 4,010	Northampton ... 61,432
Bradford 53,204	Franklin........... 45,365	Northumberland... 41,444
Bucks 64,336	Fulton............ 9,360	Perry 25,447
Butler 36,510	Greene 25,887	Philadelphia 674,022
Cambria 36,569	Huntingdon 31,251	Pike 8,436
Cameron 4,273	Indiana 36,138	Potter 11,265
Carbon 28,144	Jefferson 21,656	Schuylkill 116,428
Centre............ 34,418	Juniata 17,390	Snyder 15,606
Chester 77,805	Lancaster 121,340	Somerset 28,226
Clarion 26,537	Lawrence......... 27,298	Sullivan 6,191
Clearfield 25,741	Lebanon 34,096	Susquehanna 37,523
Clinton 23,211	Lehigh 56,796	Tioga.............. 35,097
Columbia 28,766	Luzerne 160,755	Union 15,565
Crawford 63,832	Lycoming 47,626	Venango........... 47,925

Warren 23,897	Wayne............ 33,188	Wyoming 14,585
Washington....... 48,483	Westmoreland 58,719	York 76,134
	Total..........................	3,521,791

RHODE ISLAND—Area, 1,306 square miles.

Bristol 9,421	Newport 20,050	Washington 20,097
Kent 18,595	Providence 149,190	Total....... 217,353

SOUTH CAROLINA—Area, 29,385 square miles.

Abbeville 31,129	Fairfield 19,888	Newberry 20,775
Anderson 24,049	Georgetown........ 16,161	Oconee 10,536
Barnwell 35,724	Greenville 22,262	Orangeburg....... 16,865
Beaufort.......... 34,359	Horry 10,721	Pickens........... 10,269
Charleston........ 88,863	Kershaw 11,754	Richland 23,025
Chester 18,805	Lancaster 12,087	Spartanburg 25,784
Chesterfield. 10,584	Laurens 22,536	Sumter 25,268
Clarendon 14,038	Lexington·........ 12,988	Union 19,248
Colleton 25,410	Marion 22,160	Williamsburg 15,489
Darlington 26,243	Marlborough....... 11,814	York 24,386
Edgefield 42,486	Total.......................	705,606

TENNESSEE—Area, 45,600 square miles.

Anderson 8,704	Hancock 7,148	Morgan 2,969
Bedford 24,333	Hardeman 18,074	Obion 15,584
Benton 8,234	Hardin 11,768	Overton 11,297
Bledsoe 4,870	Hawkins. 15,837	Perry 6,925
Blount............ 14,237	Haywood 25,094	Polk 7,369
Bradley........... 11,652	Henderson......... 14,217	Putnam 8,698
Campbell 7,445	Henry 20,380	Rhea 5,538
Cannon 10,502	Hickman........... 9,856	Roane 15,622
Carroll 19,447	Humphreys........ 9,326	Robertson 16,166
Carter 7,909	Jackson 12,583	Rutherford 33,289
Cheatham......... 6,678	Jefferson 19,476	Scott 4,054
Claiborne 9,321	Johnson 5,852	Sequatchie........ 2,335
Cocke............ 12,458	Knox 28,990	Sevier 11,028
Coffee 10,237	Lake.............. 2,428	Shelby 76,378
Cumberland 3,461	Lauderdale 10,838	Smith 15,994
Davidson 62,897	Lawrence 7,601	Stewart........... 12,019
Decatur 7,772	Lewis.............. 1,986	Sullivan 13,136
De Kalb........... 11,425	Lincoln 28,050	Sumner 23,711
Dickson 9,340	Macon 6,633	Tipton............ 14,884
Dyer 13,706	Madison 23,480	Union 7,605
Fayette 26,145	Marion 6,841	Van Buren........ 2,725
Fentress 4,717	Marshall 16,207	Warren 12,714
Franklin.......... 14,970	Maury 36,289	Washington........ 16,317
Gibson........... 25,666	McMinn 13,969	Wayne............ 10,209
Giles............. 32,413	McNairy 12,726	Weakley 20,755
Grainger.......... 12,421	Meigs............. 4,511	White............. 9,375
Greene............ 21,668	Monroe........... 12,589	Williamson 25,328
Grundy........... 3,250	Montgomery 24,747	Wilson............ 25,881
Hamilton 17,241	Total...................	1,258,520

TEXAS—Area, 237,504 square miles.

Anderson 9,229	Atascosa 2,915	Bandera 649
Angelina........... 3,985	Austin............. 15,087	Bastrop............ 12,290

Bee	1,082	Grayson	14,387	Milam	8,984
Bell	9,771	Grimes	13,218	Montague	890
Bexar	16,043	Guadalupe	7,282	Montgomery	6,483
Bexar District	1,077	Hamilton	733	Nacogdoches	9,614
Blanco	1,187	Hardin	1,460	Navarro	8,879
Bosque	4,981	Harris	17,375	Newton	2,187
Bowie	4,684	Harrison	13,241	Neuces	3,975
Brazoria	7,527	Hays	4,088	Orange	1,255
Brazos	9,205	Henderson	6,786	Panola	10,119
Brown	544	Hidalgo	2,387	Parker	4,186
Burleson	8,072	Hill	7,453	Polk	8,707
Burnet	3,688	Hood	2,585	Presidio	1,636
Caldwell	6,572	Hopkins	12,651	Red River	10,653
Calhoun	3,443	Houston	8,147	Refugio	2,324
Cameron	10,999	Hunt	10,291	Robertson	9,990
Chambers	1,503	Jack	694	Rusk	16,916
Cherekee	11,079	Jackson	2,278	Sabine	3,256
Coleman	347	Jasper	4,218	San Augustine	4,196
Collin	14,013	Jefferson	1,906	San Patricio	602
Colorado	8,326	Johnson	4,923	San Saba	1,425
Comal	5,283	Karnes	1,705	Shackleford	455
Comanche	1,001	Kaufman	6,895	Shelby	5,732
Cook	5,315	Kendall	1,536	Smith	16,532
Coryell	4,124	Kerr	1,042	Starr	4,154
Dallas	13,314	Kimble	72	Stephens	330
Davis	8,875	Kinney	1,204	Tarrant	5,788
Demmit	109	Lamar	15,790	Titus	11,339
Denton	7,251	Lampasas	1,344	Travis	13,153
De Witt	6,443	La Salle	69	Trinity	4,141
Duval	1,083	Lavaca	9,168	Tyler	5,010
Eastland	88	Leon	6,523	Upshur	12,039
Ellis	7,514	Liberty	4.414	Uvalde	851
El Paso	3,671	Limestone	8,591	Van Zandt	6,494
Ensinal	427	Live Oak	852	Victoria	4,860
Erath	1,801	Llano	1,379	Walker	9,776
Falls	9,851	Madison	4,061	Washington	23,104
Fannin	13,207	Marion	8,562	Webb	2,615
Fayette	16,863	Mason	678	Wharton	3,426
Fort Bend	7,114	Matagorda	3,377	Williamson	6,366
Freestone	8,139	Maverick	1,951	Wilson	2,556
Frio	309	McCulloch	173	Wise	1,450
Galveston	15,290	McLennan	13,500	Wood	6,894
Gillespie	3,566	McMullen	230	Young	135
Goliad	3,628	Medina	2,078	Zapata	1,488
Gonzales	8,951	Menard	667	Zavala	133

Total 818,579

VERMONT—Area, 10,212 square miles.

Addison	23,484	Franklin	30,291	Rutland	40,651
Bennington	21,325	Grand Isle	4,082	Washington	26,508
Caledonia	22,247	Lamoille	12,448	Windham	26,036
Chittenden	36,480	Orange	23,090	Windsor	36,063
Essex	6,811	Orleans	21,035	Total	330,551

VIRGINIA—Aera, 38,352 square miles.

County	Pop.	County	Pop.	County	Pop.
Accomack	20,409	Frederick	16,596	Nottoway	9,291
Albemarle	27,544	Giles	5,875	Orange	10,396
Alexandria	16,755	Gloucester	10,211	Page	8,462
Alleghany	3,674	Goochland	10,313	Patrick	10,161
Amelia	9,878	Grayson	9,587	Pittsylvania	31,343
Amherst	14,900	Greene	4,634	Powhatan	7,667
Appomattox	8,950	Greenville	6,362	Prince Edward	12,004
Augusta	28,763	Halifax	27,828	Prince George	7,820
Bath	3,795	Hanover	16,455	Princess Anne	8,273
Bedford	25,327	Henrico	66,179	Prince William	7,504
Bland	4,000	Henry	12,303	Pulaski	6,538
Botetourt	11,329	Highland	4,151	Rappahannock	8,261
Brunswick	13,427	Isle of Wight	8,320	Richmond	6,503
Buchanan	3,777	James City	4,425	Roanoke	9,350
Buckingham	13,371	King and Queen	9,709	Rockbridge	16,058
Campbell	28,384	King George	5,742	Rockingham	23,668
Caroline	15,128	King William	7,515	Russell	11,103
Carroll	9,147	Lancaster	5,355	Scott	13,036
Charles City	4,975	Lee	13,268	Shenandoah	14,936
Charlotte	14,513	London	20,929	Smyth	8,898
Chesterfield	18,470	Louisa	16,332	Southampton	12,285
Clarke	6,670	Lunenburg	10,403	Spottsylvania	11,728
Craig	2,942	Madison	8,670	Stafford	6,420
Culpepper	12,227	Matthews	6,200	Surry	5,585
Cumberland	8,142	Mecklenburg	21,318	Sussex	7,885
Dinwiddie	30,702	Middlesex	4,981	Tazewell	10,791
Elizabeth City	8,303	Montgomery	12,556	Warren	5,716
Essex	9,927	Nansemond	11,576	Warwick	1,672
Fairfax	12,952	Nelson	13,898	Washington	16,816
Fauquier	19,690	New Kent	4,381	Westmoreland	7,682
Floyd	9,824	Norfolk	46,702	Wise	4,785
Fluvanna	9,875	Northampton	8,046	Wythe	11,611
Franklin	18,264	Northumberland	6,863	York	7,198

Total....................................1,225,163

WEST VIRGINIA—Area, 23,000 square miles.

County	Pop.	County	Pop.	County	Pop.
Barbour	10,312	Jefferson	13,219	Pocahontas	4,067
Berkeley	14,900	Kanawha	22,349	Preston	14,555
Boone	4,553	Lewis	10,175	Putnam	7,794
Braxton	6,480	Lincoln	5,053	Raleigh	3,673
Brooke	5,464	Logan	5,124	Randolph	5,563
Cabell	6,429	Marion	12,107	Ritchie	9,055
Calhoun	2,939	Marshall	14,941	Roane	7,232
Clay	2,196	Mason	15,978	Taylor	9,367
Doddridge	7,076	McDowell	1,952	Tucker	1,907
Fayette	6,647	Mercer	7,064	Tyler	7,832
Gilmer	4,338	Mineral	6,332	Upshur	8,023
Grant	4,467	Monongalia	13,547	Wayne	7,852
Greenbrier	11,417	Monroe'	11,124	Webster	1,730
Hampshire	7,643	Morgan	4,315	Wetzel	8,595
Hancock	4,363	Nicholas	4,458	Wirt	4,804
Hardy	5,518	Ohio'	28,831	Wood	19,000
Harrison	16,714	Pendleton	6,455	Wyoming	3,171
Jackson	10,300	Pleasants	3,012	Total	442,014

96

WISCONSIN—Area, 53,924 square miles.

Adams	6,601	Green	23,611	Pierce	9,958
Ashland	221	Green Lake	13,195	Polk	3,422
Barron	538	Iowa	24,544	Portage	10,634
Bayfield	344	Jackson	7,687	Racine	26,740
Brown	25,168	Jefferson	34,040	Richland	15,731
Buffalo	11,123	Juneau	12,372	Rock	39,030
Burnett	706	Kenosha	13,147	Sauk	23,860
Calumet	12,335	Kewaunee	10,128	Shawanaw	3,166
Chippewa	8,311	La Crosse	20,297	Sheboygan	31,749
Clark	3,450	La Fayette	22,659	St. Croix	11,035
Columbia	28,802	Manitowoc	33,364	Trempealeau	10,732
Crawford	13,075	Marathon	5,885	Vernon	18,645
Dane	53,096	Marquette	8,056	Walworth	25,972
Dodge	47,035	Milwaukee	89,930	Washington	23,919
Door	4,919	Monroe	16,550	Waukesha	28,274
Douglas	1,122	Oconto	8,321	Waupacca	15,539
Dunn	9,488	Outagamie	18,430	Waushara	11,279
Eau Claire	10,769	Ozaukee	15,564	Winnebago	37,279
Fond du Lac	46,273	Pepin	4,659	Wood	3,912
Grant	37,979			Total	1,054,670

DISTRICT OF COLUMBIA—Area, 60 square miles.

Georgetown City... 11,384 Washington City...109,199 Remainder of Dist. 1,117

Total ...131,700

TERRITORIES.

ARIZONA—Area, 113,916 square miles.

Mohave	179	Yavapai	2,142	Yuma	1,621
Pima	5,716			Total	9,658

COLORADO—Area, 104,500 square miles.

Arapahoe	6,829	El Paso	987	Larimer	838
Bent	592	Fremont	1,064	Las Animas	4,276
Boulder	1,939	Gilpin	5,490	Park	447
Clear Creek	1,596	Greenwood	510	Pueblo	2,265
Conejos	2,504	Huerfano	2,250	Saguache	304
Costilla	1,779	Jefferson	2,392	Summit	258
Douglas	1,388	Lake	522	Weld	1,636
				Total	39,864

DAKOTA—Area, 50,932 square miles.

Bon Homme	608	Hutchinson	37	Todd	337
Brookings	163	Jayne	5	Union	3,507
Buffalo	246	Lincoln	712	Yankton	2,097
Charles Mix	152	Minnehaha	355	Unorganized por-	
Clay	2,621	Pembina	1,213	tion of Territory...	2,091
Deuel	37			Total	14,181

IDAHO—Area, 86,294 square miles.

Ada	2,675	Idaho	849	Oneida	1,922
Alturas	689	Lemhi	988	Owyhee	1,713
Boise	3,834	Nez Perces	1,607	Shoshone	725
		Total			14,999

MONTANA—Area, 143,776 square miles.

Beaver Head	722	Deer Lodge	4,367	Madison	2,684
Big Horn	38	Gallatin	1,578	Meagher	1,387
Choteau	517	Jefferson	1,531	Missoula	2,554
Dawson	177	Lewis and Clarke	5,040	Total	20,595

NEW MEXICO—Area, 121,201 square miles.

Bernalillo	7,591	Mora	8,056	Santa Fe	
Colfax	1,992	Rio Arriba	9,204	Socorro	6,603
Dona-Ana	5,864	San Miguel	16,058	Taos	12,079
Grant	1,143	Santa Ana	1,599	Valencia	9,993
Lincoln	1,803		Total		91,874

UTAH—Area, 84,476 square miles.

Beaver	2,007	Millard	2,753	Sevier	19
Box Elder	4,855	Morgan	1,972	Summit	2,512
Cache	8,229	Piute	82	Tooele	2,177
Davis	4,459	Rich	1,955	Utah	12,203
Iron	2,277	Rio Virgin	450	Wasatch	1,214
Juab	2,034	Salt Lake	18,337	Washington	3,064
Kane	1,513	San Pete	6,786	Weber	7,858
		Total			86,786

WASHINGTON—Area, 69,994 square miles.

Chehalis	401	Klikitat	329	Stevens	734
Clallam	408	Lewis	888	Thurston	2,246
Clarke	3,081	Mason	289	Wahkiakum	270
Cowlitz	730	Pacific	738	Walla Walla	5,300
Island	626	Pierce	1,409	Whatcom	534
Jefferson	1,268	Skamania	133	Yakima	432
King	2,120	Snohomish	599	The Disputed Islands	554
Kitsap	866		Total		23,955

WYOMING—Area, 97,883 square miles.

Albany	2,021	Laramie	2,957	Uintah	856
Carbon	1,368	Sweetwater	1,916	Total	9,118

The total for the States is........................38,113,253
"   "   Territories is........................442,730

Whole total..................38,555,983

98

ONE HUNDRED PRINCIPAL CITIES.
CENSUS OF 1870.

New York, N. Y....942,292
Philadelphia, Pa. 674,022
Brooklyn, N. Y.....396,099
St. Louis, Mo.....310,864
Chicago, Ill.......298,977
Baltimore, Md.....267,354
Boston, Mass......250,526
Cincinnati, O......216,239
New Orleans, La...191,418
San Francisco, Cal.149,473
Buffalo, N. Y......117,714
Washington, D. C..109,199
Newark, N. J......105,059
Louisville, Ky......100,753
Cleveland, O.........92,829
Pittsburg, Pa.......86,076
Jersey City, N. J....82,546
Detroit, Mich........79,577
Milwaukie, Wis.....71,440
Albany, N. Y........69,422
Providence, R. I....68,904
Rochester, N. Y.....62,386
Allegheny, Pa.......53,180
Richmond, Va.......51,038
New Haven, Ct......50,840
Charleston, S. C....48,956
Troy, N. Y..........46,465
Syracuse, N. Y......43,051
Worcester, Mass....41,105
Lowell, Mass........40,928
Memphis, Tenn.....40,226
Cambridge, Mass....39,634
Hartford, Ct........37,180
Indianapolis, Ind...36,565

Scranton, Pa........35,092
Reading, Pa........33,930
Columbus, O........33,509
Paterson, N. J.....33,579
Dayton, O...........30,473
Kansas City, Mo....32,260
Mobile, Ala.........32,034
Portland, Me........31,414
Wilmington, Del....30,841
Lawrence, Mass.....28,921
Toledo, O...........31,584
Charlestown, Mass..28,323
Lynn, Mass.........28,233
Fall River, Mass....26,766
Springfield, Mass..26,703
Nashville, Tenn.....25,865
Covington, Ky......24,505
Salem, Mass........24,117
Quincy, Ill..........24,053
Manchester, N. H...23,536
Harrisburg, Pa......23,104
Trenton, N. J.......22,874
Peoria, Ill..........22,849
Evansville, Ind......21,830
New Bedford, Mass.21,320
Oswego, N. Y.......20,910
Elizabeth, N. J.....20,832
Lancaster, Pa.......20,233
Savannah, Ga.......28,235
Hoboken, N. J......20,297
Poughkeepsie,N. Y.. 20,080
Camden, N. J.......20,045
Davenport, Ia......20,038
St. Paul, Minn.....20,031

Bridgeport, Ct......19,960
Erie, Pa............19,646
Wheeling, W. Va....19,282
Norfolk, Va.........19,229
Taunton, Mass.....18,629
Chelsea, Mass.......18,547
Dubuque, Ia........18,434
Leavenworth, Kan..17,873
Fort Wayne, Ind....17,718
Springfield, Ill......17,364
Auburn, N. Y.......17,225
Newburg, N. Y.....17,014
St. Joseph, Mo......19,565
Petersburg, Va......18,950
Atlanta, Ga.........21,789
Norwich, Ct.........16,653
Sacramento, Cal.....16,283
Omaha, Neb.........16,083
Elmira, N. Y........15,863
Gloucester, Mass....15,389
Cohoes, N. Y.......15,357
New Albany, Ind....15,396
New Brunswick,N. J.15,058
Terre Haute, Ind....16,103
Bangor, Me.........18,289
Newport, Ky........15,087
Grand Rapids, Mich.16,507
Augusta, Ga.........15,389
Burlington, Vt......14,387
Alexandria, Va......13,570
Sandusky, O........13,000
Lewiston, Me........13,600

LUCK AT LAST.

You think I'm nervous, stranger? Well, I am.
  If 'twa'n't for making silly people talk,
  I'd get right off this pokish train and walk
From here to where I'm going—Amsterdam.

That's where I live, you see. As for Lacrosse—
  (Excuse me, neighbor, I must talk or bust)—
  Since I've been there it's three years certain, just:
And now to laugh or cry is just a toss.

" Married?" Why, yes, that's where it is, you see ;
  I've telegraphed her I was strong and well,
  And coming to her ; but I didn't tell
That I was rich. I thought I'd let that be.

It's too good luck, this is, to last, you know,
  And, stranger, if I wasn't kind of rash,
  I'd bet my bottom dollar that we smash
Before—but, pshaw, excuse me, I'll go slow.

You see, when we were married, Sue and I,
  I was a good mechanic, and not poor
  Until I struck it, as I reckoned, sure,
In an invention I was working sly.

All I could make went into that concern ;
  And people called me crazy for it too,
  And said I'd better stick to what I knew ;
But folks *will* talk, and have lived to learn.

In all this world I had but one friend then,
  But she stood by me nobly, through and through,
  And said 'twould come out right at last, she knew—
One woman staunch is worth a dozen men.

'Twas tough, sometimes, though, when a loaf of bread
  Stood on the table—all the meal we had—

I should have gone alone, quite to the bad
But, through it all, my Susan kept her head

"Twas her advice that sent me off at last—
She said she'd work her fingers to the bone,
And live for twenty mortal years alone,
Rather than give it up—thank God, that's past.

A hundred thousand and a royalty
Is what I've got for going far away;
She cheered me by her letters every day;
A million could not pay such loyalty!

She knows I'm coming; but she doesn't know
That I am rich; and she will be there, too,
Dressed in her best—her best, my poor, dear Sue;
I'll bet a hundred 'twill be calico!

" *I'll* dress her now?" You bet it!—but go slow,
This luck's a heap too good to last, I fear;
I shan't believe it till I'm fairly there;
The train may smash up, easy, yet, you know.

The only reason, if it don't, will be
That I'm so strongly thinking that it will.
I'm nervous, say you? Just a little, still
The luck is none too good for Sue, you see.

Hello! we're here!—there's Sue, by all that's grand.
Stranger, excuse me, sir, but would you mind
To go ahead and tell her I'm behind?
I'm choking: see my eyes—you understand.
Janesville (Wis.) Gazette.

WM. EDGAR SIMONDS,

ATTORNEY AT LAW,

345 MAIN STREET, HARTFORD, CONN.

SOLICITOR OF

AMERICAN AND FOREIGN PATENTS.

————— ◦✦◦ —————

The writer of this work, originally prompted to this profession by natural tastes, and having enjoyed thorough scientific and legal training therefor, has been engaged, for the past six years, in soliciting letters patent for inventions, in all the patent granting countries of the world, and in the conduct of patent cases in the United States Courts, with a measure of success at once surprising and gratifying.

It has been his aim, in each case he has taken before the Patent Office, to secure for the inventor **all** *he was entitled to, sparing no pains to attain this end. He believes that he can safely refer, upon this point, to each one of the hundreds of inventors for whom he has acted.*

While the records of the Patent Office show that fully one third of all the applications made for patents are finally rejected, the proportion of final rejections upon applications made through this office, will hardly amount to one tenth. All specifications, and other papers for foreign patents, have been fully completed, ready for filing in the office for which they were designed, under his own hand—barring, sometimes, a translation—and in his own office, the significance of which statement can only be fully appreciated by a solicitor.

As in the past, so in the future, it will be his aim to render a perfect service to inventors, as regards skill, promptness, and fidelity, striving to make each case, as it comes under his hand, more perfect, if possible, than the last.

All business connected with preliminary examinations, caveats, applications for patents, reissues, interferences, extensions, disclaimers, appeals, assignments, contracts, searches, opinions, infringements, or other patent matters whatsoever, he contracts to do in the same manner. As most inventors find, sooner or later, good work in patent matters is worth everything, poor work worse than worthless.

The writer does not offer himself as a competitor, in the matter of prices, with those solicitors who take work on any terms they can get, yet he knows that his charges are much less *than those of other solicitors who are competent to perform, and do perform the same quality of work.*

He will be pleased, upon request made, to forward a pamphlet circular, which is explicit in the matter of terms, etc., both for home and foreign patents.

If you have a difficult or rejected case, you are invited to submit it for his opinion as to the chances of success, which opinion will be given, usually, without charge, and a fee named upon which the case will be undertaken.

With reference to suits at law upon patents, attention is drawn to the following professional card:

W. E. SIMONDS,

ATTORNEY AT LAW,

Practitioner in the U. S. Courts.

PATENT CASES A SPECIALTY.

ERRATA.

———

On page 12, line 2, the words "as low" should follow the word "fixed."

On page 25, line 10, "proportion" should read "proposition."

On page 47, under head of "Undivided Interests," the words "that it is probably lawful," should be inserted immediately after the word "understand," in line 2.

On page 48, line 15, the word "USE," should follow the word "MAKE."

On page 74, line 9, omit the word "such."

INDEX.

W.E. SIMONDS

SOLICITOR OF PATENTS

HARTFORD CT.